Pathology

for

DEATH INVESTIGATORS

Pathology
for
DEATH INVESTIGATORS

JAY DIX

ISBN: 0-9663422-8-3

Printed in the United States of America

Cover Design: Paul L. Cary

CONTENTS

FOREWORD

This book is intended for those individuals who investigate death. The text, in outline format, consists of the important points for each of the different types of deaths investigators will encounter. The color photographs in the atlas pictorially illustrate the specific causes of death with individual, as well as case examples. Hopefully, a better understanding of the different causes will promote more complete and thorough death investigation.

JD

PART I

DISCUSSION

POSTMORTEM INTERVAL AND DECOMPOSITION

POSTMORTEM INTERVAL

Determining the time of death, or the interval between the time of death and when a body is found (i.e., postmortem interval) can only be estimated. Unless a death is witnessed, or a watch breaks during a traumatic incident, the exact time of death cannot be determined.

Rigor Mortis (Rigidity) — The stiffening of muscles after death.

A. Begins within 1–3 hours after death.

B. The higher the body temperature, the quicker the onset.

C. The higher the environmental temperature, the quicker the onset.

D. The more strenuous the physical activity prior to death, the quicker the onset.

E. At 70–75 °F, the body is completely stiff in 10–12 hours.

F. All muscles of the body begin to stiffen at the same time after death. Muscle groups appear to stiffen at different rates because of their different sizes. For example, stiffness becomes apparent sooner in the jaw than it does in the knees or elbows. Therefore, the examiner should first check the jaw, then the elbows, and lastly the knees.

G. The body will remain stiff for 24–36 hours before the muscles begin to loosen.

H. When a body stiffens it remains in that position until rigor passes or a joint is physically moved and rigor is broken.

Livor Mortis (Lividity) — The discoloration of the body after death.

A. The blood settles by gravity into small blood vessels in the dependent areas of the body.

   B. The normal color of lividity is purple.
   C. Some areas will not become discolored because bones and tissues are compressed against a hard surface.
   D. Lividity is noticeable approximately 1 hour after death.
   E. Livor mortis becomes "fixed" in about 8 hours.
   F. Lividity present in a nondependent areas indicates the body has been moved after death.
   G. Livor mortis is more difficult to see in dark-skinned individuals.
   H. Lividity loses its distinctness as decomposition develops.
   I. Carbon monoxide, cyanide, hypothermia, and refrigeration will cause bright red lividity.
   J. People who die from extensive blood loss have a very light or non-existent lividity.

Body Cooling (Algor Mortis) — Cooling of the body after death.
   A. The body cools from its normal internal temperature (98.6 °F) to the surrounding environmental temperature.
   B. The rate of the cooling is not exact.
   C. At an environmental temperature of 70–75 °F, the body cools at approximately 1½ °F per hour.
   D. More rapid cooling takes place in cold environments.
   E. If body temperature is measured at the scene, the environmental temperature should be measured, at least twice.

Other
   A. Eyes cloud over within a couple of hours after death in most people.
   B. The potassium content in eye fluid may help determine the postmortem interval, but the interpretation is not consistently reliable.
   C. Stomach contents can be used to determine the last meal eaten, but is generally not a reliable indicator of the time of death.

DECOMPOSITION

General
   A. In general, as rigor passes, the skin begins to turn green. The green discoloration is usually seen in the abdomen first.

B. As discoloration occurs, the body will begin to swell as bacteria in the body form gas.

C. Bodies that are buried in earth, submerged in water, left in the hot sun, or placed in a cool basement will not look the same after the same postmortem interval.

D. As the body bloats from the gas, blood begins to break down and stain the vessels. The vessels just beneath the skin will become visible due to the staining process. The pattern that is formed is called "subcutaneous marbling."

E. As bloating continues, hair and skin readily slip off the body.

F. As internal pressure builds, blood and bodily fluids come out of body orifices. This is called "purging."

G. Skeletonization may occur within a few weeks if the environmental temperature is high. In contrast, a body exposed to a 65 ° environment may not skeletonize for many months or years.

H. Decomposition may be asymmetric. That is, decomposition may occur more rapidly in one part of a body than in another. This is especially true in areas of injury. If a man is struck on the head and bleeding occurs only in that area, decomposition may be much more advanced on the head than on the remainder of the body. Flies are attracted to injured areas where they feed on exposed blood proteins and cause accelerated decomposition.

Adipocere — The hardening of the soft tissue (turns into fat) beneath the skin.

A. Occurs in wet and moist climates. Cold temperatures inhibit the bacteria that normally proliferate and form gas.

B. Commonly seen in bodies that have been submerged in water during the winter months.

C. Usually takes a minimum of a few weeks to develop.

D. Once developed it will keep the body in a relatively preserved state for many months or years.

E. Unlike normal decompositional changes, there is no green discoloration or significant bloating.

F. The exterior of the body remains white and the outermost layers of the skin slip off.

G. For bodies totally submerged in water, adipocere will be evenly distributed over all body surfaces.

H. Those bodies found in bags and other containers may have an asymmetric distribution of adipocere.

Mummification — The skin loses water and turns leatherlike.

A. Mummification occurs in hot and dry environments.

B. The body dehydrates and bacterial proliferation is minimal.

C. The skin becomes dark, dried, and leathery.

D. The soft tissue beneath the skin begins to decompose as the skin dries and hardens.

E. After a few weeks, the entire body may appear preserved. There will be considerable soft tissue shrinkage.

SCENE INVESTIGATION

A. Clues about the time of death may also be found at the scene.

B. Insect larvae on the body can be collected and saved in alcohol. An entomologist will be able to state how long the larvae have been on the body.

C. Plants discovered under or near a body can be sent to a botanist for examination. The botanist can classify the specimen as to the time of year it would normally be present, and how much time elapsed to reach that particular growth stage.

D. Information from a scene not associated with a body may also be critical in estimating the time of death. Was the mail picked up? Were the lights on? Was food being prepared? Was a major appliance on? Was there any indication as to activities an individual was performing, had completed, or was contemplating? How was the person dressed?

Utilizing all available information from a scene and performing a careful external and internal examination of a body is the best way to make an educated estimate as to the time of death.

FIREARM INJURIES

HANDGUNS AND RIFLES

A. Rifles and handguns fire ammunition or cartridges composed of a primer, gunpowder or propellant, and a bullet or projectile.

B. The primer at the base of the cartridge is ignited after the firing pin strikes. The primer ignites the gunpowder and this explosion sends the bullet down the barrel.

C. Some of the gunpowder, primer, and metal from the barrel may be deposited on the victim's clothing, skin, or other objects. The presence of this material on the victim's clothing or skin is what aids the examiner in determining the distance between the gun and the victim.

D. Primer material may be deposited on the skin of the shooter.

E. Handguns and rifles are manufactured with cuts in the barrels, called grooves. The grooves alternate with "lands" (the raised portion between the cuts), which result in markings on the bullet as it passes down the barrel. These markings allow the bullet to be matched with the weapon that fired it.

Gunpowder — Exits the muzzle in two forms:

1. Completely burned gunpowder, called "soot" or "fouling." This material can be easily washed off the skin.

2. Particles of burning and unburned powder that can either become embedded in the skin or bounce off the skin, leaving an abrasion. These marks on the skin are called "tattooing" or "stippling."

Range of Fire — The presence or absence of gunpowder on the victim's clothing or skin indicates whether the gunshot wound was contact (loose or tight), close, intermediate (medium), or distant.

A. **Tight contact**
   1. All of the gunpowder residue is on the edges or in the depths of a wound.
   2. There may be searing or burning of wound margins.
   3. The surrounding skin may be red because of carbon monoxide gas produced by burning powder.
   4. There is often tearing of the skin around the entrance site in head wounds because pressure builds up and blows the skin back toward the muzzle of the gun.
   5. There is usually a partial pattern of the muzzle around the edges of a tight contact wound.

   There may be soot around a tight contact wound if there is clothing between the gun and the skin.

B. **Loose contact** — Gunpowder may escape between the skin and muzzle if the gun is not held tightly against the skin. This deposited soot around the edges of the wound can be easily washed off the skin.

C. **Close range** — Close range gunshot wounds occur at muzzle-to-target distances of usually less than 12 inches. Both soot and stippling are present.

D. **Intermediate range** — These wounds occur at muzzle-to-target distances of approximately 12 inches to 3 feet. There is no soot, only stippling of the skin.

E. **Distant wounds** — No soot or stippling on the skin or clothing.

The presence of clothing may prevent gunpowder from getting to the skin. It is important that all clothing be retained for testing if needed.

The above definitions and distances are not specific to any weapon. They are only guidelines. The best method of determining an accurate distance is to test fire the same weapon and the same ammunition used in the shooting.

Entrance Wounds

   A. Tend to be circular defects with a thin rim of abrasion caused by a bullet scraping the skin as it enters the body.
   B. May have unusual shapes if the skin surfaces are not flat. This is especially true of gunshot wounds to the face.

Exit Wounds

A. Exit wounds may be circular like entrance wounds, but they are often irregular in shape. They may be slitlike or have ragged edges.

B. They usually do not have a rim of abrasion like entrance wounds unless the victim's skin is pressed against another object. The presence of an abrasion around the wound would make it a "shored" exit wound.

C. Skin around an exit wound may also be discolored because of underlying bleeding in the soft tissues.

The scene must be examined for bullets and cartridges. Care must be observed when moving the victim because bullets may be caught in clothing. The bullet may slow considerably after traveling through bone and the elastic skin of the body.

Victims of gunshot wounds should be x-rayed in order to locate bullets or bullet jackets. Jackets may separate from their underlying lead core as they pass into the body.

SHOTGUNS

A. Shotguns have smooth bores with no lands or grooves.

B. Pellets recovered from a body cannot be matched to a particular shotgun.

C. Distant determinations are easier in shotgun deaths because of pellet spread.

D. Shotguns usually fire pellets, but they can also fire slugs. These solid projectiles are similar to large bullets except they do not travel as far and are stopped or slowed as they pass through the target. Some of these have been matched to particular weapons.

The pathologist should recover all bullets, jackets, and large fragments from the body. The course and direction of each shot should be described. At least 10–15 pellets from each shotgun blast should be recovered for the ballistics' expert to determine shot size.

CHAPTER
3

BLUNT TRAUMA

GENERAL CHARACTERISTICS

A blunt trauma injury is any injury not caused by a gun or sharp object. The characteristic injuries of blunt trauma are contusions, abrasions, and lacerations. Abrasions occur externally whereas contusions and lacerations may be external or internal.

Contusions (Bruises) — Discolorations of the skin caused by bleeding into the tissues from ruptured blood vessels.

A. There is no way to determine exactly how much force was used to produce a contusion.

B. The age of a contusion is difficult to determine because of the great variability of a body's reaction to trauma.

C. People with blood disorders and liver disease may develop contusions more easily than healthy individuals.

D. As healing occurs, a contusion changes color from blue or red, to red–blue, to green, to brown, and finally yellow. These color changes, however, may appear out of order and may overlap.

E. There is no way to know how long each color stage will last. For example, a recent contusion will have a brown tinge.

F. Sometimes taking a sample of the bruise and looking at it under the microscope may allow the differentiation between newer and older contusions.

G. Older people bruise more easily than young people.

Abrasions (Scrapes) — Skin scraped away by friction.

A. A wound may be either deep or superficial depending on the force and the coarseness of the surface that caused the abrasion.

B. A person who slides across pavement might have a deeper and rougher wound than a person who slides across a rug.

C. Occasionally, the direction of the force can be determined. If one end or side of an abrasion has margins with raised skin, the force originated from the opposite side.

Lacerations (Tears) — A splitting of the skin from blunt trauma.

A. Many tears are associated with both contusions and abrasions. For example, a blow to the head with a hammer may cause tearing of the scalp with adjacent abrasions. If blood escapes into the surrounding tissues, the skin can also be bruised.

B. A laceration must be distinguished from a cutting injury. A laceration, especially of the head, usually has bridges of tissue connecting one side of the wound to the other. Cutting and incised wounds have no tissue bridges because a sharp object cuts the wound cleanly from the top of the wound to the bottom.

Deaths due to blunt trauma may have some or none of the above external signs of trauma. This is particularly true of fatal blows to the abdomen. When the belly is struck, the skin stretches and the soft tissue collapses. The pressure is absorbed on the inside of the body and not externally. It is not uncommon to see fatal tears in abdominal organs in children who have been struck and not see any external contusions.

Pattern Injuries

A. Most weapons don't leave a pattern on the skin.

B. Patterns are more common in areas of the body where bone is under the point of impact. They tend to be more commonly seen on the head.

C. There are many weapons that leave a pattern. Some of the more common instruments that leave a pattern include hammers, wrenches, batons, bats, flashlights, fingers, boots, shoes, and belts.

D. Any long and thin object has a good chance of leaving a pattern.

E. Rarely can a pattern be matched specifically to an object. The examiner will usually say that the characteristics of a particular weapon are or are not consistent with the pattern.

Bite mark injuries can usually be differentiated from injuries caused by other weapons. Teeth tend to leave distinctive marks and patterns.

An odontologist may be able to positively match a bite mark to a particular person.

BLUNT HEAD TRAUMA

A. Any blow to the scalp or face may produce contusions, lacerations, and abrasions.
B. There may be no external signs of trauma to the head if a person was struck on a full head of hair.
C. External injuries are not necessary for a death to be caused by head trauma.

Battle's Sign — A bluish discoloration of the skin behind the ear that occurs from blood leaking under the scalp after a skull fracture.

Spectacle Hemorrhage (Raccoon's Eyes)

A. A discoloration of the tissues around the eyes due to fractures of the skull, broken nose, or impacts to the eyes.
B. The hemorrhages may involve one or both eyes and may be mistakenly interpreted as indicating that the decedent was struck about the face and eyes.

Subscalpular Hemorrhages

A. A blow to the scalp will reveal a hemorrhage on the underneath surface.
B. Individual hemorrhages mean separate blows.
C. The presence of a subscalpular hemorrhage only implies there was a blow to the head. It doesn't necessarily mean there is underlying damage to the brain.

Fractures of the Skull

A. Any crack in the skull is a fracture.
B. Fractures come in all shapes and sizes.
C. It is difficult to prove how many blows there were to the head based on the number of fractures. A more accurate count is provided by counting the number of distinct subscalpular hemorrhages.
D. Occasionally, the type of fracture suggests the type of weapon involved. For example, circular and depressed fractures measur-

ing approximately 1–2 inches in diameter suggest a hammer as the weapon.

Intracranial Bleeding

A. **Epidural hemorrhage** — Bleeding directly under the skull that is almost always associated with a skull fracture.

B. **Subdural hemorrhage** — Bleeding under the dura (the thick tissue membrane covering the brain). Blood accumulates after veins are ruptured. The bleeding tends to accumulate over a slower period of time than in an epidural hemorrhage.

C. **Subarachnoid hemorrhage** — Bleeding on the surface of the brain. This is the most common hemorrhage occurring after head trauma. Though it also happens after the rupture of an aneurysm, a ruptured aneurysm is rarely the result of trauma.

Except for the bleeding that occurs with ruptured aneurysms, all of the above types of intracranial bleeding are signs that blunt trauma occurred. Blunt trauma may not necessarily be the cause of death. For example, a person could have fractures of the skull and all three types of brain hemorrhages, but still die from a stab wound to the heart.

Brain Contusions

A. These are similar to bruises on the skin.

B. They are caused by broken blood vessels from trauma. They are red–brown and are located on the surface of the brain.

Coup and Contrecoup Injuries

A. **Coup** — Caused by a moving object hitting a stationary head. The injuries are directly under the point of impact. This type of injury is seen when a person is hit by a hammer or some other hard object.

B. **Contrecoup** — Caused by a moving head hitting a stationary object. The injuries are located opposite the site of impact. This type of injury may be seen when a man falls down the stairs and strikes his head.

MOTOR VEHICLE INJURIES

OCCUPANT INJURIES

A. Blunt trauma is the cause of death in nearly all motor vehicle accidents.

B. A person can die in an accident and have no external injuries. This is especially common since the advent of air bags.

C. During frontal or side impacts, the occupant's body will receive injuries as if it moved toward the site of impact. This occurs more commonly when the person is unrestrained.

D. Injuries occur from impacts with other objects, sudden deceleration, and intrusions by other vehicles. The driver generally has steering wheel impacts, while the passenger does not. Both may hit the dashboard, windshield, and rearview mirror.

E. Each injury pattern is governed by what is struck.

F. Certain injuries are particularly common and characteristic:

1. Injuries to the chest from a blunt impact with a steering wheel may leave very few external marks, but result in a tear of the aorta. This occurs because the body decelerates rapidly as it strikes the steering wheel and the aorta rips as it stretches.

2. The front windshield is composed of two pieces of glass bonded together. The glass may shatter on impact, but the two layers remain bonded. Injuries from hitting the windshield vary from contusions and abrasions to lacerations and open skull fractures.

3. Side windows are made of tempered glass and shatter into numerous small fragments. These fragments cause a characteristic "dicing" pattern of cuts and abrasions on the face, shoulders or arms.

4. The presence of dicing abrasions is one method of determining an occupant's position. A driver should have the dicing injuries on the left side of his body while passengers should have them on the right.

G. Other common injuries are fractures of the knees, femura (thigh bones), and lower legs caused by hitting the dashboard or by the legs being caught under the seat. Needless to say, high-speed collisions can cause multiple severe injuries.

H. Extensive skull fractures, brain contusions, subscalpular hemorrhages, facial lacerations, and numerous other contusions and abrasions to the head and face may also be present.

I. Common injuries to the trunk include rib and pelvic fractures and lacerations of the liver, spleen, and other abdominal organs. Lacerations of internal chest organs may occur without associated rib fractures.

J. Straplike abrasions on the shoulder and hip areas may be produced by seat belts. Severe neck trauma may be caused by whiplash.

K. If any of the occupants are ejected during a crash, the injuries may be quite variable and very severe. Head trauma is common in these situations. Ejected occupants may die from striking other objects such as the roadway. The vehicle may roll over the ejected individual causing compression asphyxia as well as crushing injuries.

PEDESTRIAN INJURIES

Many pedestrians struck by motor vehicles have characteristic injury patterns. It is important to study these patterns and compare them with the description of how the accident occurred.

A. **Primary Injuries**

1. These injuries occur during the initial impact of the vehicle with the pedestrian. Common locations include the legs and hips. The locations of primary sites of impact may be considerably different in children than in adults.
2. Children tend to be run over and adults tend to be thrown to the side of the roadway or lifted up because they have higher centers of gravity than do children.
3. The distance between the initial impact fracture site on the legs and the heels should be measured. These distances may

give some indication of the vehicle's bumper height at the moment of impact.

4. Bumper fractures may have a triangular shape, the apex of which points in the direction the vehicle was traveling.
5. The examination of the decedent's clothing may reveal paint chips, glass, and other parts of the vehicle. These small pieces of evidence may be all that is needed to connect a particular vehicle to the body. Clothing must always be saved and examined in any pedestrian–motor vehicle fatality.

B. **Secondary Injuries**

1. When struck, the pedestrian may subsequently impact the vehicle, ground, or other object.
2. An adult commonly strikes the hood, top, or windshield of the vehicle.
3. The decedent's blood, tissue, or hair may be transferred to the vehicle. This transference may also occur on the ground, trees, or other objects not connected with the vehicle.
4. The distance from the initial impact to the final resting place of the body may be considerable in high-speed impacts. The measurement of this distance aids the accident reconstructionist to calculate the speed the vehicle was traveling at the moment of impact.
5. Other destructive injuries may occur if the body is struck by a second or third vehicle after the initial impact. The damage may be impressive if the vehicles are traveling at high speeds. In such cases, evaluation of the initial impact site on the body may be difficult.

CUTTING, STABBING, AND CHOPPING WOUNDS

CUTTING (INCISED) WOUNDS

A. An incised wound (cut) is made by a sharp instrument.
B. By definition, it is longer on the skin surface than its depth within the body.
C. The edges of the wound tend to be sharp and usually not ragged or abraded.
D. The surrounding skin is usually undamaged.
E. Within the wound, tissue bridges do not connect one side of the wound to the other, as seen in a laceration.
F. Virtually any sharp object may cause an incised wound.

STAB WOUNDS

A. A stab wound is deeper than it is wide.
B. The depth of the stab wound should be determined by direct examination and not by probing.
C. Probing the wound before opening the body is fraught with potential errors. Both the direction and the depth of the wound can be miscalculated by inserting an instrument into the wound.

Entrance Wounds

A. The ends of the entrance stab wound are called angles.
B. The angles of the wound may be blunt or sharp depending on the weapon.
C. A single-edged blade will create one blunt angle and one sharp angle.

D. Knives with two cutting edges will cause two sharp angles.

E. The wounds caused by homemade sharpened weapons may be more difficult to analyze because the angles may be sharp, dull, or a mixture of the two.

F. Angles may dry out if examination of the body is delayed. If this occurs, evaluation of the angles may be difficult or impossible.

G. Some stab wounds are cause by rounded weapons such as ice picks or screwdrivers. There may be no angles when these types of weapons are used.

Determining Manner

A. The types and locations of the injuries may suggest the manner of death.

B. Multiple incised and/or stab wounds of the neck, face, and extremities (so-called "defense" wounds) are usually caused by an assailant; therefore the manner is homicide.

C. Multiple incised wounds of varying depths on the neck or wrists suggest a suicide.

D. Superficial incised wounds adjacent to a deep incised wound are referred to as hesitation marks and are characteristic of self-inflicted injuries.

E. A body sustaining many stab and incised wounds is characteristic of a situation known as "overkill." This usually occurs in a highly emotional setting such as one involving sex or drugs.

Weapon Determination

A. Care must be taken when relating the size of an entrance wound on the skin surface to the dimensions of a weapon.

B. The skin's elasticity can distort the shape of a wound. For example, a weapon causing the same angle of entry in both the chest and abdomen may cause a horizontal defect in the abdomen and a diagonal wound in the chest.

C. The width and length of a weapon's blade may be estimated by analyzing a stab wound. A 1-inch wide blade, for example, causes a 1-inch wide wound on the skin surface if a knife is inserted and pulled straight out. If either the victim or assailant moves, the external wound may be longer.

D. The length of the wound track in the body may be longer than the blade length if the weapon is thrust deeply into the body and the tissue springs back when the weapon is removed.

E. The same weapon can also cause different types of stab, incised, and puncture wounds.

CHOP WOUNDS

A. Heavier weapons with sharp blades may cause a combination of incised wounds and blunt trauma.

B. The mechanism of death may either be exsanguination or complications of blunt trauma.

Cause of Death

A. Most victims of sharp force trauma die from bleeding, internally or externally.

B. Healthy individuals can lose almost a third of their blood volume and survive.

C. A person with underlying heart or other disease may die after losing much less blood.

D. It is relatively easy to estimate and/or measure the amount of blood in the body at autopsy.

E. It is more difficult to estimate the amount of blood loss at the scene. For example, a cup of blood spread throughout a room may appear as if much more than a cup was lost from the body.

F. Both the amount of blood loss from the body and the estimated amount at the scene should be taken into account when determining if the death was due to exsanguination.

ASPHYXIA AND DROWNING

ASPHYXIA

Asphyxia means lack of oxygen to the brain. Following are the different ways a person can asphyxiate:
  A. Compression of the neck (hanging and strangulation)
  B. Blockage of the airway (suffocation, aspiration, gagging)
  C. Compression of the chest (postural asphyxia)
  D. Chemical ingestion and inhalation
  E. Lack of available oxygen
  F. Autoerotic suffocation
  G. Drowning

A. Compression of the Neck (Hanging and Strangulation)

1. In hanging (usually suicide), the neck can be compressed by any object. The usual ligatures are ropes or articles of clothing.
2. Pressure on the neck usually causes death by blocking the blood vessels, not the airway (larynx or trachea).
3. Only 4 or 5 pounds of pressure are needed to block the veins on the sides of the neck to cause asphyxiation.
4. More pressure is needed to compress the deeper arteries, such as the carotid, in the same location.
5. The neck can also be compressed manually by an assailant's hands (manual strangulation or throttling). An assailant must compress either the airway or the blood vessels in order to render the victim unconscious.
6. One sign of manual strangulation is fracture of the hyoid bone which is located above the larynx (voice box).
7. The time it takes to render an individual unconscious is quite variable (seconds to over a minute). Usually, once a victim

becomes unconscious, pressure must be continued in order to cause death.

8. Signs of trauma to the neck are generally evident in manual strangulation and hanging.

    i. There may be contusions or abrasions but rarely lacerations. An object used to compress the neck often leaves an abraded, imprinted mark.

    ii. If the ligature is thin like a rope, the depressed mark on the neck is usually apparent and sometimes the pattern can be matched to the particular ligature.

    iii. If the ligature is wide like a towel or shirt there is usually no distinct pattern.

    iv. Superficial fingernail cuts may be found on the neck of a strangulation victim. These cuts are more likely from the victim as he/she attempts to remove the assailant's hands.

    v. Petechiae

        a. These pinpoint hemorrhages in the eyes are caused by pressure buildup in the small blood vessels called capillaries.

        b. Almost always present in victims of manual strangulation.

        c. Seen on both the bulbs of the eyes and inside the eyelids.

        d. May also be found on the face, especially the forehead, and around the eyes.

        e. Not always present in suicidal hanging, but commonly seen in violent accidental chest compression such as occurs traffic accidents.

        f. Not specific for asphyxia and may be seen in cases of sudden natural death, and occasionally in CPR attempts.

B. Blockage of the Airway (Suffocation, Aspiration, Gagging)

1. Asphyxiation occurs when the airway is blocked and oxygen cannot get into the lungs.

2. Any object, such as a pillow or a hand, can be placed over the mouth and cause suffocation.

3. An unchewed peanut or parts of toys can become lodged in an infant or child's airway.

4. Someone gagged by an assailant may suffocate if the gag swells and air exchange is prevented.

5. Individuals without teeth or with a history of strokes or other debilitating diseases may have trouble chewing and aspirate food into the airway.

6. People under the influence of alcohol are also more likely to aspirate. There may be no signs of trauma in these types of deaths.

C. **Compression of the Chest (Postural Asphyxia)**

1. Postural asphyxiation occurs when there is an inability to move one's chest.

2. Commonly seen during motor vehicle accidents when the vehicle overturns on a victim or a driver becomes trapped between the steering wheel and seat.

3. There may be surprisingly few injuries in these cases.

4. Petechiae tend to be present in such deaths.

D. **Chemical Ingestion and Inhalation**

1. Two types — carbon monoxide (CO) and cyanide poisoning.

2. Both of these substances interfere with oxygen delivery to the tissues.

3. Carbon monoxide is formed when anything containing carbon, such as wood or gas, burns. This molecule competes with and blocks oxygen from attaching itself to red blood cells, thereby preventing oxygen from getting into the blood system. Carbon monoxide can incapacitate a person within minutes.

4. Cyanide prevents respiration on a cellular level and can kill a person quicker than carbon monoxide. Like carbon monoxide, cyanide causes livor mortis to be cherry red. Cyanide may smell like bitter almonds.

E. **Lack of Available Oxygen**

1. If the atmosphere's oxygen is replaced by another chemical or gas, or if a person's red blood cells are unable to deliver oxygen to bodily tissues, a person will asphyxiate.

2. Depletion of atmospheric oxygen usually occurs in relatively closed environments, such as improperly vented sewers, chemical storage tanks, or mine shafts.

3. It is common to encounter multiple deaths in such scenes because fumes and lack of oxygen can also overcome rescuers.

F. Autoerotic Suffocation

1. Autoerotic suffocation can result from the purposeful attempt to reduce blood flow to the brain by compressing the neck during masturbation.
2. Any object that compresses the neck can be used.
3. Most of the time a towel or some other soft object is placed between the ligature and the neck to prevent visible scrapes or bruises.
4. The diagnosis is readily made at the scene because the decedent is usually completely or partially naked and pornographic material is nearby.
5. Often there is evidence of repeated behavior at the scene, such as worn grooves in the rafters where ropes or pulleys have been placed.
6. The manner of death is accidental.

DROWNING

1. A diagnosis by excluding other causes of death.
2. There may be injuries as the result of being in the water. Tears and scrapes of the skin from impacts against rocks, trees, boats or other objects are common.
3. Occasionally, marine life (more often in salt water than in fresh water) may feed on the skin of the face, especially around the mouth, nose, and ears.
4. Abrasions may be found on the forehead, knees, and backs of hands from a body scraping against the bottom of the lake, river, pond, or pool.
5. There may be no external signs of trauma.
6. Froth in the nose and mouth is usually present.
7. Wrinkling of the skin on the hands and feet is typical.
8. Petechiae are not usually present; however, they may be seen in "forced" drowning.
9. People drowning in salt water typically have heavy lungs filled with water.
10. People drowning in fresh water may or may not have water in their lungs.

PEDIATRIC FORENSIC PATHOLOGY

BATTERED CHILD SYNDROME

A. These children have a history of being repeatedly beaten by a caregiver.
B. The injuries occur over periods of weeks, months, and years.
C. It is common to see healing injuries such as rib fractures and contusions in addition to the recent injuries that caused death.
D. Pathologists routinely see internal injuries to the head or abdomen without the corresponding external signs of blunt trauma.
E. Pathologists cannot age or date contusions with certainty because of individual variations in healing.
F. The pathologist will determine if there are any signs of sexual abuse.
G. Many children who are killed from a beating are not chronically abused. They may be killed on the spur of the moment by an exasperated caretaker who is unable to cope with their crying or unruly behavior.
H. All injuries should be photographed.

SHAKEN BABY

A. There may be no external signs of trauma if a child is shaken to death.
B. There may be contusions on the arms or chest where the infant was held while being shaken.
C. The cause of death in these cases usually results from nerve damage inside the brain.
D. Findings from the internal examination include:
   1. **Retinal hemorrhage** — This is bleeding in, on, or under the retina inside the eyes. It may be seen before death with the aid of an ophthalmoscope or after death by the pathologist.

2. **Optic nerve hemorrhage** — Bleeding around the optic nerves which is seen inside the head at the autopsy.
3. **Subdural hemorrhage** — Rarely are more than a few milliliters of blood present. It tends to be over the top and both sides of the brain. A blow to the head might be suspected if there is a considerable amount of subdural bleeding.
4. **Subarachnoid hemorrhage** — Usually only a very small amount is present.
5. **Diffuse axonal injury** — This is the cause of death in a shaken infant. The injuries can only be seen with the aid of a microscope.

All of the above do not need to be present in a case of shaking.

E. Some pathologists feel a child must be both struck and shaken for death to occur.

F. Sometimes the diagnosis "shaken impact syndrome" is rendered. This diagnosis is appropriate when there are obvious external or internal blunt impact injuries.

G. A child usually becomes unconscious or noticeably abnormal within seconds or minutes of the violent act.

H. There may be a delayed onset of symptoms or signs of a problem if the child lives after shaking.

NEGLECT

A. Children do not need to be battered for a medical examiner to rule a death a homicide.

B. Child abuse and death can result from neglect. For example, if a child is not fed or if a child is left in a harmful situation (left unattended in a hot car), death may occur.

C. The diagnosis of a malnourished or starved child is easy to make. The child's weight is significantly low for the age and the child has the typical "concentration camp" appearance. The eyes are sunken and the skin is loose because of a lack of soft tissue fat.

D. The medical record should be reviewed to compare the last recorded body weight with the weight at autopsy. A sudden loss of weight must be explained.

E. It is more difficult to make the diagnosis of dehydration than it is to make the diagnosis of starvation.

F. If present, eye fluid (vitreous fluid) can be checked for salt content to prove dehydration.

SUDDEN INFANT DEATH SYNDROME (CRIB DEATH OR SIDS)

A. Each year almost 3,000 children die of SIDS.
B. The cause of death in these babies is unknown.
C. The incidence is less among babies who are placed on their backs when put to bed.
D. The peak age for these deaths is from about 3 weeks to 4 months.
E. A diagnosis of SIDS requires a complete autopsy and scene investigation and can only be made if both the scene and the autopsy are unremarkable or negative.
F. Bloody fluid or froth in the nose may be the only external finding at autopsy. This fluid may cause considerably spotting on the sheet or mattress at the scene.
G. Internally, most babies have petechiae of the thymus or other organs.

SUFFOCATION

A. This may be very difficult to determine in an infant.
B. There may be no external or internal signs of trauma.
C. Petechiae are rarely seen as they are in adults.
D. The autopsy is usually negative; therefore the scene investigation is vitally important.
E. The common types of suffocation in an infant include:
   1. Intentional pushing of the head face down in bedding.
   2. Intentional blockage of the nose and mouth.
   3. Intentional compression of the chest.
   4. Accidental suffocation by a parent when sleeping together (overlaying).
   5. Accidental rebreathing carbon dioxide while sleeping face down in bedding.
   6. Accidental postural or positional compression.

ELECTROCUTION, LIGHTNING, THERMAL, AND ENVIRONMENTAL INJURIES

ELECTROCUTION

A. Not always an easy diagnosis to make (the history and circumstances of death are very important).

B. Low-voltage deaths frequently cause no injuries on the body. If present, they may be small red, black, or white lesions.

C. High-voltage deaths are easier to diagnose because of obvious burns.

D. The cause of death from electrocution is related to the amount of amperage flowing through a body.

E. Most deaths occur from contact with alternating currents, especially in homes with low voltages (110 or 220).

F. There needs to be a complete circuit from the power source to the ground for death to occur.

G. A person will not become electrocuted if insulated from the ground.

H. The direction the path takes in the body determines whether or not the shock will be fatal. Current through the heart and brain are the causes of death.

I. The extent of external wound damage is dependent upon the amount of current and its duration.

J. Clothing may be damaged so it must be retained for examination.

K. Burning clothes may secondarily damage the skin.

LIGHTNING

A. Lightning may kill by either a direct or an indirect strike.
B. Injuries may be slight to nonexistent or quite impressive.
C. The victim usually dies as a result of heart stoppage.
D. Metal on the clothing or body may heat up and cause secondary injuries.
E. Occasionally, a red fernlike pattern may develop on the skin; however, it may disappear within hours of the death.

FIRE DEATHS AND THERMAL INJURIES

A. Most fire-related deaths are the result of carbon monoxide (CO) poisoning and not direct thermal injury.
B. Exposure to CO can be fatal within minutes.
C. Thermal effects to the body may be slight or severe.
D. The degree of thermal damage to the body does not dictate how long a person survived during a fire.
E. The extent of damage to the body depends on the body's proximity to the fire and whether or not the decedent was exposed to the flames.
F. The most important factor in any fire death investigation is determining whether an individual was dead before a fire started (suspected homicide). This is determined by examining the airway for the inhalation of smoke and measuring CO content in the blood.
G. The evaluation of the airway and collection of blood should be performed in the morgue.
H. An explosion may cause such a rapid death that the CO will be negative.
I. The amount of CO in a person's system at the time of death is quite variable.
J. Death at low CO concentrations may be associated with underlying disease or intoxication.
K. Heavy smokers may have CO concentrations slightly over 10 percent before the fire, but higher levels indicate they were alive at the time of the fire.
L. Individuals may die later in the hospital from complications such as inhalation injuries to the airways, infections, and fluid and elec-

trolyte disorders. Skin burns may range from partial or full thickness to charring and incineration.

M. Bodies from fire deaths should be x-rayed so that foreign objects will not be overlooked.

N. Blood can usually be obtained from a body no matter how badly it is burned.

O. CO will cause cherry red livor mortis.

P. Heat artifacts include:
   1. Changes in height and weight.
   2. Hair color changes. Brown hair may become red and blonde may become gray. Black hair does not change color.
   3. Thermal fractures. These may be difficult to differentiate from antemortem fractures.
   4. Skin splits with evisceration of organs.

ENVIRONMENTAL INJURIES

Hyperthermia

A. The definition of hyperthermia is a body temperature of at least 108 °F.

B. The most important finding at autopsy is high body temperature.

C. There are no specific injuries in this cause of death.

D. Malignant hyperthermia is a syndrome that develops in people who react to certain drugs, such a phenothiazines (thorazine) or halothane.

E. Older people may succumb to heat during summer months because an underlying disease contributes to their inability to cope with heat, or because their dwellings may not have an appropriate cooling system.

F. The use of cocaine and methamphetamine is also associated with hyperthermia. In some cases there is a genetic predisposition toward developing "malignant" hyperthermia.

G. Drug screens should always be performed.

Hypothermia

A. Hypothermia occurs more commonly in those individuals who have underlying disease or are incapacitated, such as under the influence of alcohol.

B. People can die from improperly heated homes or apartments or if they are caught outside in the cold. Alcoholics can become hypothermic if they fall asleep in the cold while inebriated. Nursing home patients can succumb to the cold after becoming confused and walking outdoors during winter months.

C. At autopsy, there are usually no external signs of trauma unless the individual was rendered incapacitated by an injury before dying from the cold. Internally, there may be small hemorrhages in the stomach.

D. Toxicological studies are essential hypothermia-related deaths.

E. For unknown reasons, some people dying of hypothermia begin to undress before death. This is called "paradoxical undressing." Finding a naked woman dead in the cold may lead investigators to mistakenly believe she was sexually assaulted.

ALCOHOL AND DRUGS

ETHYL ALCOHOL (ETHANOL)

A. The legal limit to be considered driving under the influence of alcohol in most states is 80–100 mg% (0.8–.010 g%). This is an equivalent amount of alcohol in approximately 4–5 glasses of 12% wine or 4–5 12-ounce cans of beer.

B. A blood alcohol level does not represent the amount of alcohol consumed during an evening or a day, but is simply the amount of alcohol in the system at the time of the blood sample is taken.

C. Ethanol is usually eliminated from the body at a constant rate.

D. Approximately one ounce of pure alcohol is metabolized every hour or approximately 0.02 grams % per hour.

E. The physical effects of chronic alcohol use:

1. Alcohol affects most organ systems, especially the liver (cirrhosis). Other organs involved are the pancreas, heart, brain, and muscles.

2. Cirrhosis of the liver may lead to bleeding from the mouth and rectum.

3. Cancer is the second leading cause of death in alcoholics (heart and blood vessel) and the rate of cancer within this group is 10 times higher than that of the general population.

4. Chronic alcoholics may die suddenly without any alcohol in their system and the only finding at autopsy may be an accumulation of fat in the liver.

5. A death from any disease caused by chronic drinking is considered natural.

6. Chronic alcoholics are prone to hypothermia. Dying from the cold is an accidental death.

7. Rapid consumption of alcohol followed by death is an accidental death.

DRUGS

General

A. The investigation of death by suspected drug abuse is slightly different than for other types of death because a pathologist must rely on toxicology results in order to make the diagnosis.

B. An autopsy usually does not reveal a specific cause of death unless signs of previous abuse are present, such as needle track marks and scars from skin-popping.

C. An autopsy may reveal a bolus of pills within the stomach in a suicide victim who did not live long after ingestion, or plastic packages (often condoms) filled with drugs as seen in "body packers" or "mules" who transport drugs.

D. There may be considerable white froth or blood-tinged material in the nose and airways. Internally, pulmonary edema is usually present in a drug overdose death.

E. Other findings, such as heart disease, may also be present which may contribute to death.

F. The most important analysis needed from a postmortem exam is the drug screen. Blood, bile, urine, liver, brain, and gastric contents can all be studied.

G. The fluid in the eye (vitreous humor) may also be screened for drugs of abuse; however, it should not be the only specimen submitted. Vitreous is a good specimen for measuring alcohol.

H. A toxic concentration of a drug in a decedent's system does not always indicate a cause of death. The decedent's past history of drug abuse must be taken into account.

I. Chronic drug abusers can tolerate higher concentrations of their drug of choice.

Stimulants

A. Cocaine is a potent, naturally occurring stimulant and one of the most commonly abused stimulants in this country.

B. Cocaine can be sniffed, smoked (crack), or taken intravenously.

C. Cocaine is quickly metabolized in the blood stream to its metabolite benzoylecgonine.

D. Methamphetamine (and amphetamine) may be taken orally, intravenously, or smoked (ice).

E. Sudden death associated with cocaine and methamphetamine use may be due to a cardiac arrhythmia, heart attack, or ruptured blood vessels.

F. Cocaine and methamphetamine have been associated with bizarre and irrational behavior (delirium or psychosis) and hyperthermia.

Hypnotics, Depressants, and Analgesics

A. Heroin, morphine, and painkillers such as Talwin, Dilaudid, and codeine are commonly encountered.

B. The mechanism of death from these classes of drugs is usually respiratory depression.

C. Except in suicidal overdoses, in which there may be retention of pills in the stomach, there are no specific signs of an overdose at autopsy.

D. Froth in the airways and pulmonary edema may be present.

Hallucinogens

A. LSD is rarely the sole cause of death.

B. LSD may be a contributing factor in death because it causes irrational and careless behavior.

C. PCP (phencyclidine), unlike LSD, can kill.

D. PCP is both a stimulant and a depressant and has been associated with bizarre outbursts similar to the stimulant frenzy described with cocaine.

Miscellaneous

A. GHB and Ecstasy have recently been associated with numerous deaths.

B. People do not die of marijuana overdoses.

C. Children commonly overdose on adult doses of over-the-counter and prescription medicines.

SUDDEN NATURAL DEATH

CARDIOVASCULAR DISEASE
(HEART AND BLOOD VESSEL DISEASE)

Arteriosclerotic (Hardening of the Arteries) Heart Disease

A. Heart disease is the leading cause of death and sudden death in this country.

B. Atherosclerosis is a type of arteriosclerosis that is characterized by a thickening of the blood vessel wall by fat and other material. This accumulation leads to a plugging of the blood vessel.

C. The most common cause of sudden death is atherosclerosis of the coronary arteries.

D. Atherosclerotic coronary heart disease leads to heart attacks (myocardial infarctions) and arrhythmias (abnormal heart beats).

E. The pathologist can only see a heart attack that is many hours old. A sudden death from a heart attack or an arrhythmia will not leave a visibly damaged area of the heart wall.

F. Cardiac arrhythmia is also the final event of other kinds of natural diseases. Since it can't be determined visually, it is diagnosed by excluding all other possibilities.

G. The amount of coronary artery disease necessary to cause sudden death is quite variable from one person to another. For example, a man with known, severe, triple-vessel coronary artery disease may live for many years, while one with only moderate, single-vessel disease may die suddenly without having any previous signs or symptoms. The reason why this variability exists is unknown.

A medical examiner who views an elderly person dead in bed without signs of foul play will probably rule the death to be secondary to arteriosclerotic heart disease since this is the number one cause of sudden natural death. This diagnosis may be rendered whether or not an autopsy is performed.

Hypertensive (High Blood Pressure) Heart Disease

A. An enlarged heart with thickened walls and no other significant disease is usually regarded as a hypertensive heart.

B. In many instances, however, there will be no history of high blood pressure.

C. Sudden death in people with hypertensive heart disease may be due to an arrhythmia or to one of the other complications of hypertensive cardiovascular disease, such as a rupture of the aorta or bleeding in the brain.

Other Types of Heart Disease

A. Less common forms of heart disease that cause sudden death include congenital and valvular heart disease, cardiomyopathy, and myocarditis.

B. There are numerous congenital abnormalities of the heart that may cause sudden death. Single coronary arteries and abnormal anatomic distributions of the coronaries are relatively common.

C. Many severe congenital problems may be discovered at birth or not until much later.

D. Diseases of the valves may be present from birth or develop later.

E. Infections of the valves are not uncommon in drug abusers.

F. Cardiomyopathies are diseases of the heart wall, having both known and unknown causes. One example, asymmetrical hypertrophy (uneven thickening of the heart walls), may cause sudden death at a young age, often during exercise.

G. Sudden unexpected deaths may also occur from infections, such as a complication from a viral illness.

VASCULAR (BLOOD VESSEL) DISEASE

A. **Ruptured Cerebral Aneurysm (Ballooned-Out Blood Vessel)**

1. These are enlarged blood vessels in the brain that rupture.

2. Rupture of these aneurysms may cause sudden death without warning symptoms. Most people do not survive a ruptured berry aneurysm.

3. A rupture may occur at a time of stress, during a sudden increase in blood pressure, or during a nonstressful occasion.
4. A ruptured vessel may also be discovered at autopsy in an individual who has fallen. In this unusual circumstance, the rupture preceded the fall and was not caused by the fall.

B. **Pulmonary (Lungs) Thromboemboli (Blood Clots)**
   1. Most originate in the deep veins of the lower legs.
   2. They may also arise in veins of the pelvis or lower abdomen, especially during pregnancy, or in extremities at the site of a previous injury.
   3. Fatal blood clots most commonly develop in individuals who become bedridden after surgical procedures and in anyone whose activity level suddenly decreases.
   4. Blood clots that cause death are usually discovered in the large blood vessels that take blood from the heart to the lungs.
   5. The victim can die very suddenly if the blood clots are large.

C. **Ruptures of the Aorta**
   1. The aorta may rupture as a consequence of an aneurysm or the wall may split apart. Aneurysms in the aorta are common because of the buildup of fatty deposits.
   2. Almost all elderly individuals have some of this disease by the time they die.
   3. This disease may cause the aortic wall to weaken, balloon-out, and rupture.
   4. Death is usually quick after a rupture because of the tremendous amount of blood lost in such a short time.
   5. The other type of rupture that can occur in the aorta is called a dissection. This occurs as the wall of the vessel splits apart.
   6. Dissections of the aorta are associated with high blood pressure, cocaine abuse, and some congenital abnormalities.

CHRONIC ALCOHOLISM

A. Chronic alcoholics may die suddenly, presumably from an arrhythmia.
B. They may also have dilated cardiomyopathy due to the toxic effects of alcohol.

C. The liver commonly contains fat and there may be alcohol in the blood.

D. Death due to chronic alcoholism is considered natural.

E. Death from acute alcohol intoxication, however, with a markedly elevated blood alcohol concentration, is considered an accident.

CENTRAL NERVOUS SYSTEM DISORDERS

A. Very few disorders of the CNS cause sudden and unexpected death.

B. Brain tumors can cause sudden death, but patients usually present to a physician with symptoms of their disease prior to death.

C. Occasionally, a child dies suddenly from an unsuspected and undiagnosed rapidly growing brain tumor.

D. Meningitis may present with nonspecific symptoms such as a headache and may not be diagnosed in an emergency room. Within hours, the symptoms may progress rapidly and cause death before adequate medical attention is obtained.

E. The most common disorder of the CNS that causes a sudden death is a seizure.

F. Seizures may be caused by injuries at birth or later on in life. Some causes are unknown. If someone dies as the result of a seizure that was caused by a blow to the head, death is considered an accident. This is because the blow to the head started the train of events that led to the person's death.

G. Identification of a gross or microscopic abnormality in the brain that triggers a seizure is rarely found because seizures are caused by abnormal electrical activity. Clearly, a decedent's history and a complete drug screen are important when making a diagnosis of death due to a seizure.

RESPIRATORY (LUNG) DISORDERS

A. Sudden deaths from respiratory disorders are usually due to infections.

B. Infants and the elderly may succumb to pneumonia very suddenly without exhibiting significant symptoms.

C. Bacteria may secondarily infect an already established viral infection of the airway.

D. People with AIDS or cancer readily develop respiratory infections, but these disorders are usually expected.

THE NEGATIVE AUTOPSY

A. At least 1–2% of the autopsies in a busy forensic jurisdiction will be negative and the deaths will be ruled undetermined.

B. Negative autopsies tend to occur in younger individuals without previous injuries or medical problems.

C. What do pathologists do if the autopsy is negative? First, they make sure a complete scene investigation is performed. Then they review all autopsy findings, including microscopic studies and the results of a complete drug screen. If this fails to reveal a cause, the pathologist will usually make the ruling of "unknown natural causes."

THE AUTOPSY

GENERAL

A. A forensic pathologist or a pathologist who is knowledgeable about trauma and sudden death should conduct the autopsy.

B. All findings should be described in an autopsy report that is completed after the examination.

C. A pathologist may dictate the findings at the time of the exam or document them on a worksheet and dictate them later.

D. Injuries in suspicious cases and homicides should be photographed.

E. Some jurisdictions also videotape the autopsy.

F. All information from a case must be retained in the decedent's case file for future study and review, if needed.

G. The most important information determined at the autopsy is the cause of death.

H. The manner of death may not be obvious after examining the body. Therefore, scene investigation is essential in determining the manner of death.

I. Besides documenting signs of injuries and natural diseases, the pathologist may need to collect specimens for drug screens and for evidence that may be important in homicide investigations.

SPECIMEN COLLECTION

A. **Blood**

1. Blood must be collected for drug screens, blood typing, and DNA comparisons.

2. Blood should be refrigerated and may even be frozen.

3. Blood should be collected in every case—it is always better to have it and not use it than discover later that it was needed but never obtained.

B. **Urine**

1. Urine is good for screening many drugs, especially drugs of abuse.

2. If a urine screen is negative, the blood may not have to be analyzed.

C. **Anal, Vaginal, and Oral Swabs**

1. Cottons swabs are used to collect seminal fluid and sperm in suspected cases of rape.

2. Slides from swabs should be made to check for sperm and then specimens should be air-dried prior to packaging.

D. **Foreign Material** — hairs, threads, fragments of wood, metal, and any other foreign material should be collected in homicides, or suspected homicides.

E. **Clothing**

1. Every article of clothing in homicides and suspicious cases should be dried and bagged in paper bags.

2. Clothing should not be cut off the body in homicides.

F. **Hair**

1. Head hair samples are routinely taken in homicides.

2. Pubic hair samples are submitted if a sexual assault is suspected.

3. Hair samples should be taken from more than one site.

4. Combings of the pubic hair in suspected sexual assault cases should be submitted separately.

5. Many of the above specimens, including blood samples, are taken and collected together in a prepackaged sexual assault kit.

G. **Vitreous Humor**

1. This fluid is good for screening certain drugs, especially alcohol.

2. It is also used to measure glucose and electrolytes, especially sodium, chloride, urea, and creatinine.

H. **Other**

1. Crime scene technicians or their representatives should attend an autopsy and help the pathologist collect evidence.

2. All physical evidence and biological specimens should be placed in separate containers.

3. Each container should be labeled with the pathologist's or investigator's name, date, autopsy number, and type of specimen.

4. A chain of custody begins at the time the specimens are collected and turned over to law enforcement.

THE PROCEDURE

A. After an extensive external examination, the pathologist usually begins an autopsy with the standard "Y" shaped incision. The short arms of the "Y" begin at the shoulders, meet at the breast. and the incision continues in a straight line to the pubis.

B. The skin is then reflected away from the chest and abdominal regions. The chest plate (ribs and sternum) is exposed and removed by a saw.

C. The sac around the heart (pericardial sac) is opened and blood is removed for toxicological studies. Peripheral sites are the preferred location for obtaining blood for drug screens.

D. The organs are then removed all at once (Rokitansky method) or individually (Virchow method).

E. An assistant usually removes the brain. An incision is made from behind one ear and then extended across the top of the head down to behind the other ear. The scalp is reflected both forwards and backwards to expose the skull. The top of the skull is removed with a saw and the brain is exposed. The brain is removed and evaluated.

F. There is no one proper method of performing an autopsy. A complete examination is recommended because a decedent may have more than one potential cause of death.

G. The pathologist samples internal organs for microscopic examination when necessary.

H. The cause of death is usually determined at the conclusion of the autopsy, i.e., at the end of the gross examination; however, the results of microscopic analyses and toxicology may be needed before the cause of death can be determined.

THE REPORT

A. A final autopsy report is generated when all the data, including the results of the drug screens are completed.

B. Each report should have an injury section separate from other external findings.

C. A list of final diagnoses and opinions or comments should also be separate from the main body of the report.

D. There should be no editorializing or interpretations in the body of the report. These comments can be made in a separate opinion or comment section.

DECEDENT IDENTIFICATION

POSITIVE IDENTIFICATION

A. **Visual**

　1. The most common method of positive identification is visual.

　2. Some jurisdictions require the next of kin to make the identification in person, while others will alleviate some of the relative's trauma by allowing the family member to view a photograph of the face or body.

　3. Other jurisdictions suggest the relatives not look at the body until after it has been prepared for viewing at the funeral home.

　4. Numerous injuries and decompositional changes may prevent visual identification.

B. **Fingerprints** — All individuals have unique fingerprints. Millions are on file in a national data bank and can be readily retrieved by most law enforcement jurisdictions.

C. **Dental**

　1. An excellent means of positive identification, unless the decedent is edentulous.

　2. Many pathologists can make the comparisons, however, an odontologist should analyze difficult cases.

　3. Most often a decedent with a complete set of dentures can be identified. The technician who made the dentures may have put the decedent's name or some other form of personal identification on the denture.

D. **X-Rays**

　1. Antemortem studies can be used for postmortem comparisons.

　2. Both radiologists and forensic pathologists make these comparisons.

3. A radiologist should be consulted if the case is difficult.
4. X-rays of the skull and the pelvis tend to be the best for comparison.
5. The skull has sinuses (cavities) in the forehead area that are specific to each individual.
6. A chest x-ray is not as good as the skull and pelvis x-rays for comparison.

E. DNA

1. All individuals except identical twins have unique DNA.
2. Any material with cells containing DNA can be used for comparison.
3. Blood, hair, semen, teeth, and other tissue may be used.

PRESUMPTIVE IDENTIFICATION

A. Skeletal Remains

1. Skeletal remains should be studied by a forensic anthropologist.
2. The anthropologist can determine age, gender, and race.
3. Some anthropologists are also quite proficient in determining causes of injury to the bones.

B. Clothing

1. The style, size, and make of clothing are commonly used to make a presumptive identification.
2. Relatives or friends may remember what the person was last wearing.
3. Many clothes will decompose along with the rest of the body or will be destroyed if the body is burned.

C. X-rays

1. Antemortem x-rays do not ensure a positive identification.
2. A presumptive identification can be made if the x-rays are consistent with those of the decedent and there is no reason to believe they are of another person.

D. Physical Features

1. Tattoos, scars, birthmarks, the absence of organs from surgical procedures, and other physical anomalies are helpful in making identifications.

2. The presence or absence of any of these characteristics may also be helpful in eliminating a possible match and making an identification.

E. **Circumstances Surrounding Death**

1. Identifications may be impossible to make based on the few remains discovered at the scene.

2. The circumstances in which the remains are discovered may allow an identification to be made. For example, if only a few pieces of a body are located in a burned-out house, it may be impossible to make a positive identification. However, if the owner of the house was last seen in the house, or if there is no reason to believe the remains are those of someone else, a presumptive identification of the owner can still be made.

CHAPTER 13

CAUSE, MECHANISM, AND MANNER OF DEATH

Cause — The cause of death is the injury or disease that begins the process that leads to death.

A. **Proximate Cause** — The initial event, such as gunshot wound or blunt trauma to the head.

B. **Immediate Cause** — The last event prior to death, such as infection or bleeding.

Important — the length of time between the proximate and immediate cause does not change the final diagnosis or cause of death as long as there is an unbroken chain of events between the two. The time frame may be minutes, days, or years. A complete history and investigation are critical in making sure the train of events between the proximate and immediate cause are not broken.

EXAMPLE: A 50-year-old man had been in a car accident when he was 30 years old. The accident left him paralyzed from the waist down. For the past 20 years since the accident he has had problems with bladder infections. His last hospital admission was for treatment of a bladder infection. The infection spread and he died.

The *immediate cause* of this man's death is infection. The *proximate cause* of his death was related to the injuries he received in the traffic accident 20 years prior to his death. The manner of his death is accident.

Mechanism — The biochemical or physiologic abnormality resulting in death.

The mechanism of death in the above case is shock from the infection. Other common mechanisms of sudden death include arrhythmias (abnormal heart beats) of the heart and exsanguination (bleeding).

Manner — The manner of death is the circumstance surrounding the death.

Traditionally, the manner is classified as one of the following: homicide, suicide, accident, natural, or undetermined. In the above case of the man dying from constant bladder infections, the manner of death is accident.

The ruling of homicide means one person killed another. It does not imply criminality or intent. This is left to the courts. Someone can die of a heart attack and the manner still can be homicide. It is a homicide if an assailant points a gun at someone during a robbery and the victim becomes excited and dies of a heart attack. In this circumstance, the assailant had the unfortunate luck of pointing his gun at someone with a bad heart. The rule is, "you take your victim as you find him."

PART II

ATLAS

Photo 1. Sudden death. Chronic alcoholics can die suddenly. This alcoholic died while standing at the sink. *See next photo.*

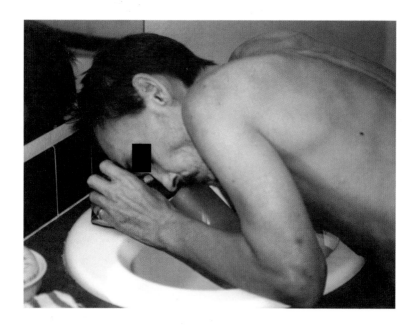

Photo 2. A close-up view shows that he was getting a drink of water when he died. His death was extremely sudden, indicating a probable abnormal heartbeat (arrhythmia). *See next photo.*

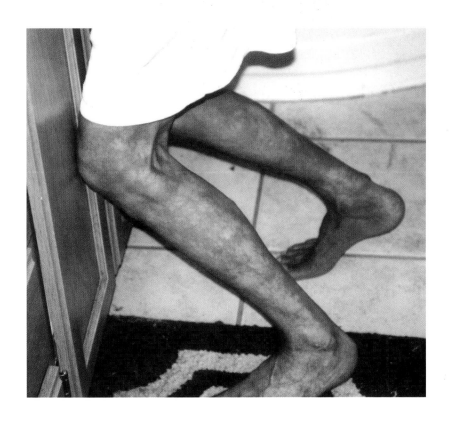

Photo 3. Lividity has settled in his legs. This is consistent with him dying in an upright position. *See next photo.*

Photo 4. Numerous bottles of alcohol were in the apartment. *See next photo.*

Photo 5. His body was in complete rigor. If the room temperature were 70–75 °F, this would indicate he had been dead for at least 10 hours. If he had been discovered on the floor in this position, the investigator would have known that his body had been moved because his arms are not in contact with the floor. People can die with their arms in the air, but they fall to the floor shortly after death. *See next photo.*

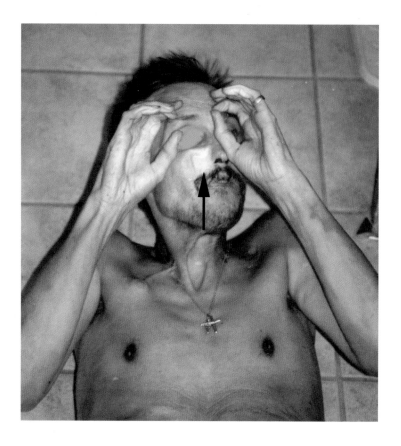

Photo 6. A close-up view of his face reveals a white pressure mark *(arrow)* that occurred after death.

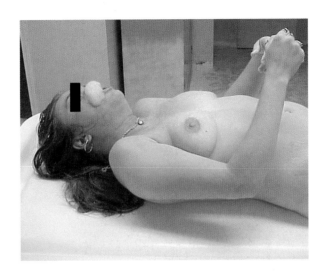

Photo 7. This is fixed rigidity in a drowning victim. Notice the foam in her mouth.

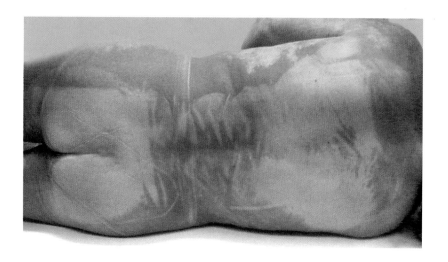

Photo 8. This man has posterior lividity. The areas on the buttocks and back are pale because blood is prevented from settling in those areas due to contact with the surface on which he is lying. Lividity begins approximately 1 hour after death and becomes "fixed" after nearly 8 hours. The normal color of lividity is purple. Red lividity occurs in cold environments, and in carbon monoxide and cyanide poisonings. Lividity may also turn red during decomposition.

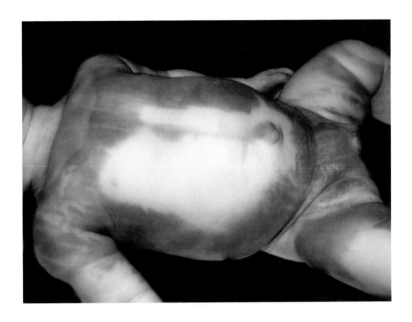

Photo 9. The anterior lividity on this baby's chest and abdomen suggests he was face down when death occurred. *See next photo.*

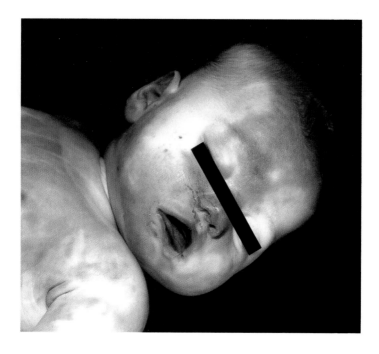

Photo 10. The pale areas on his face suggest his head may have been wedged. The possibility of a suffocation death should be investigated.

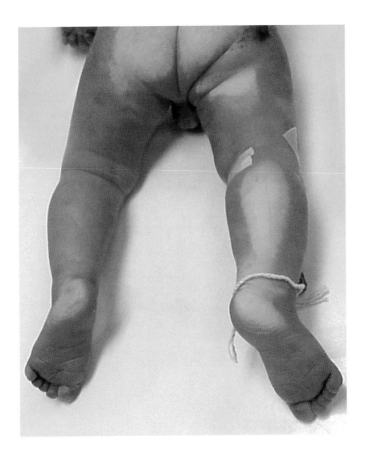

Photo 11. Lividity will turn red after refrigeration.

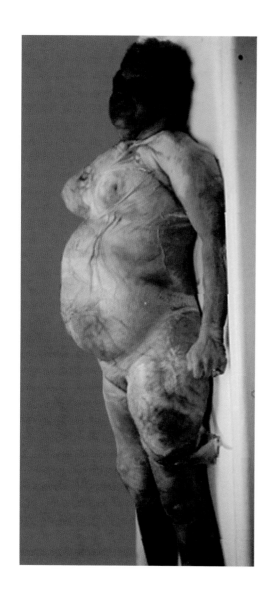

Photo 12. Diffuse skin slippage in this lady occurred after she was out in the hot sun for 8–10 hours before her body was discovered.

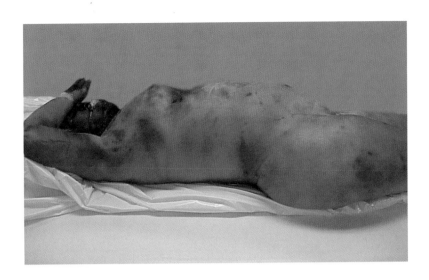

Photo 13. This woman's body is green from decomposition and yellow because of mummification.

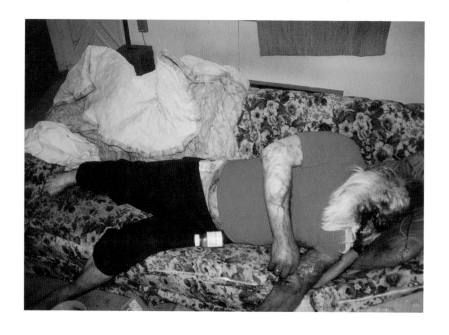

Photo 14. This man died of a seizure. His body was not discovered for at least 2 days. *See next photo.*

Photo 15. Purging is evident. The bubbles from the purging spattered his pillow. The spattering made it appear that he had been injured.

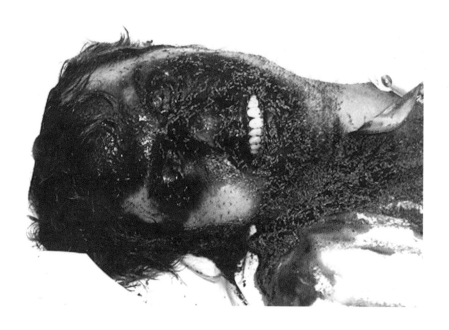

Photo 16. This man, with maggots and decompositional changes of the face, was discovered lying face down on the ground. The rest of his body was not decomposed. Any determination of postmortem interval should be evaluated by looking at the areas with the least decomposition.

Photo 17. This woman was missing for 3–4 months and was last seen in November. She floated down the Missouri River over 125 miles before her body came to rest. Her tissues had undergone adipocere change that indicated she had been in cold water for many months.

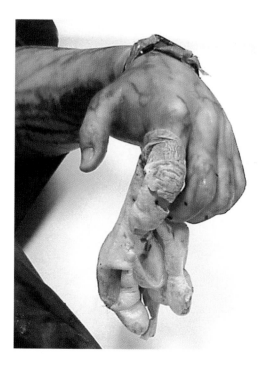

Photo 18. The skin on this hand slipped off due to heat and decomposition. This individual's fingerprints are on the skin that slipped off and not on the hand. Only the skin is needed for identification.

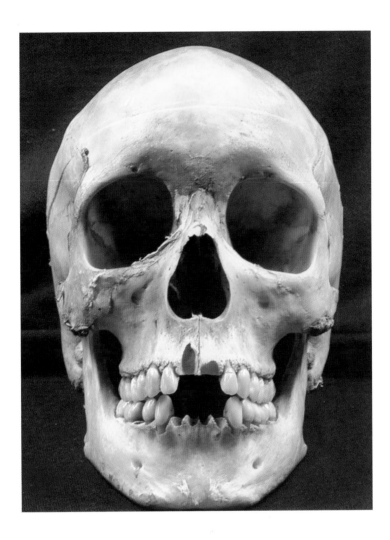

Photo 19. This skull is a skull from a woman who was killed and sunk in water. Most of the tissue was gone. The skull was sent to the anthropologist for facial reconstruction. *See next photo.*

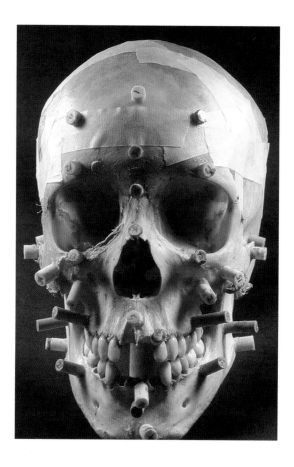

Photo 20. Tissue depths are determined based on the race of the individual. *See next photo.*

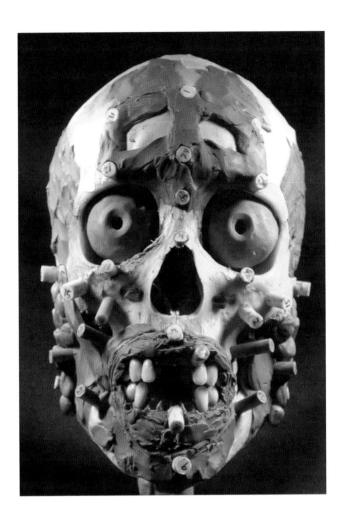

Photo 21. Clay is then placed over the skull based on the predetermined tissue depths. *See next photo.*

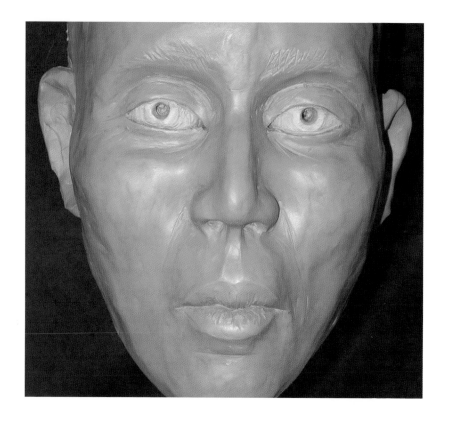

Photo 22. This is the completed face. The parts of the face that are difficult to determine are the nose, ears, and hairstyle. *See next photo.*

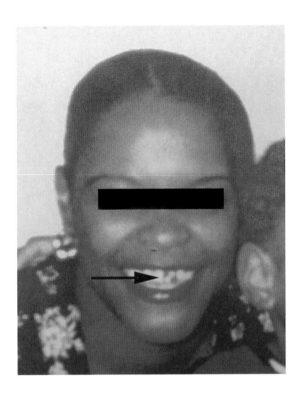

Photo 23. This is a woman who was identified based on the facial reconstruction. A false upper incisor *(arrow)* aided in the identification. Dental records were not available.

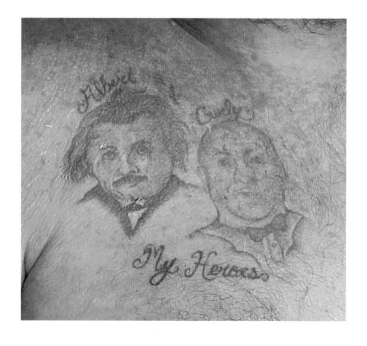

Photo 24. Identification may also be made with distinctive tattoos, such as this one.

Photo 25. Distinctive clothing is also helpful when making identifications.

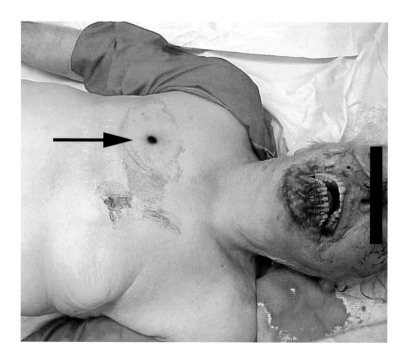

Photo 26. Shot in the chest *(arrow)* by her husband, this woman was left on the bedroom floor for 2 days before authorities found her. *See next photo.*

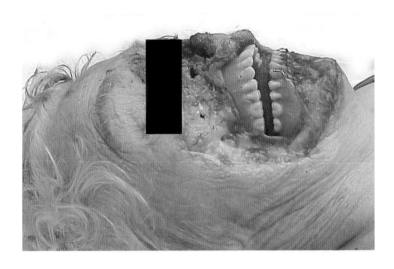

Photo 27. The family cat had eaten her face. Postmortem damage by animals is called anthropophagia.

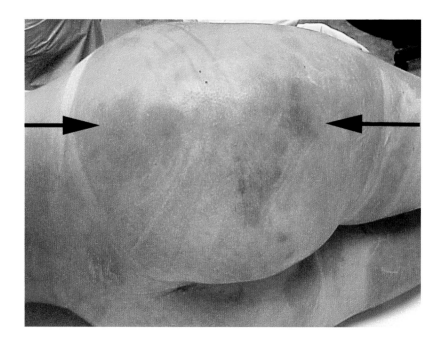

Photo 28. Bruises *(arrows)* are discolorations of the skin occurring from blood vessels that rupture after blunt trauma. *See next photo.*

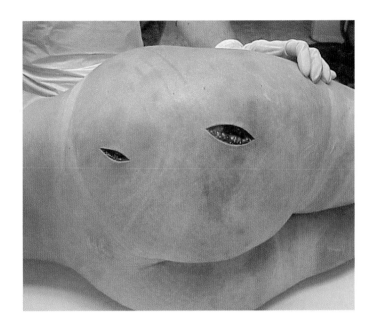

Photo 29. Incising a contusion will reveal blood in the fat. There will be no hemorrhage in the fat if the skin discoloration is caused by lividity.

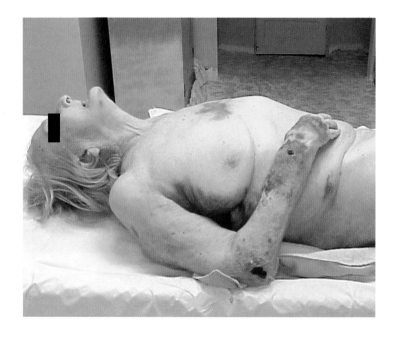

Photo 30. This elderly woman's death was suspicious because there were bruises on her arms and trunk. *See next photo.*

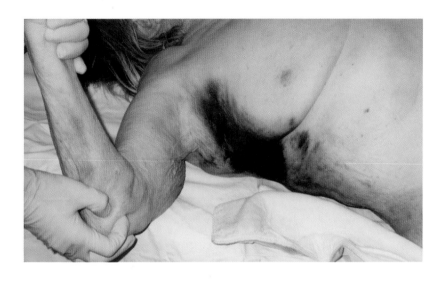

Photo 31. The extensive bruising under her arms were postmortem injuries caused by strapping her body to a cart for transportation to the morgue.

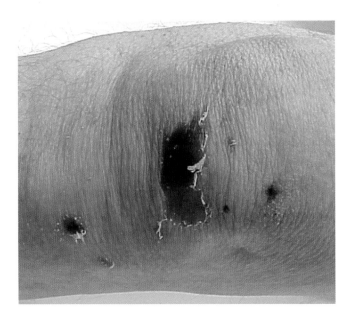

Photo 32. The heaped-up margins in an abrasion will indicate the direction of the force. In this case the force came from the left side because the skin margins are heaped-up on the right.

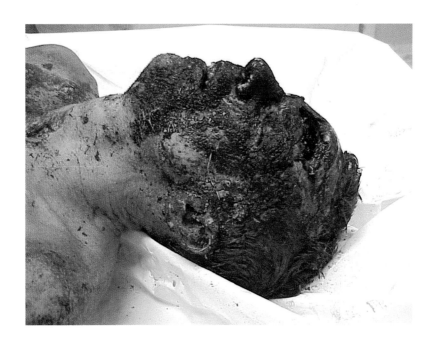

Photo 33. This man was found dead in a field near some horses. He was a veterinarian. There was a large wound on the forehead. *See next photo.*

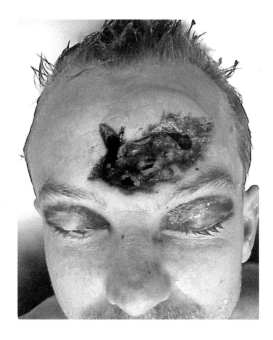

Photo 34. After his head was cleaned, the impressiveness of the wound was apparent. His eyes were blackened because of the skull fractures and not from direct impact to his eyes. The blood seeped through the fractures into the tissues around the eyes. These blackened eyes are called spectacle hemorrhages or raccoon's eyes. *See next photo.*

Photo 35. When first discovered, the man was lying on the ground dressed only in his shoes and socks. Apparently, he was shoeing one of his horses when he was kicked and dragged.

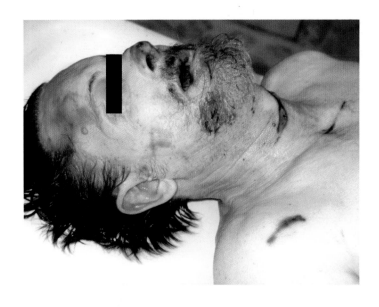

Photo 36. This man was beaten and died from head trauma. The right side of his face revealed no pattern injuries. *See next photo.*

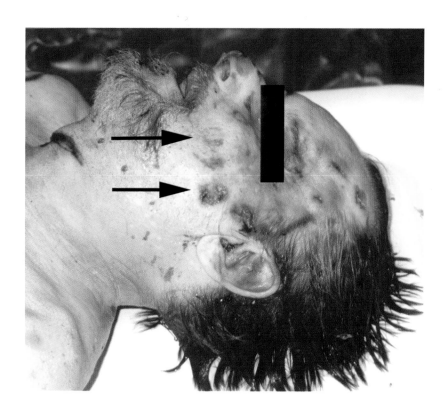

Photo 37. Examination of the left side of his face revealed some circular patterns *(arrows). See next photo.*

Photo 38. A circular saw with blood on it was found at the scene. The marks on the man's face were caused by the wrench used to change the blade depth *(arrow)*.

Photo 39. This worker was discovered at the factory where he was employed. Since multiple safety devices were deactivated, his death is clearly a suicide.

Photo 40. A train decapitated this man. He was last seen the night before arguing with some associates. A witness said he was struck once on the side of the face before he left the group. The amount of blood at the scene around his head suggests he was alive at the time of decapitation. *See next photo.*

Photo 41. How he ended up on the track is a mystery. During the night, the railroad cars that ran over his head were pulled from the siding by an engine. Speculation is that he passed out on the track or against one of the wheels. The autopsy revealed a bruise on the right side of his face and drugs in his system. *See next photo.*

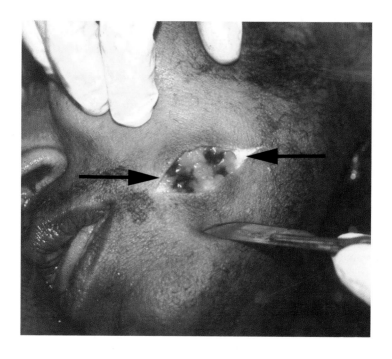

Photo 42. An incision into the bruised area on the left side of his jaw *(arrow)* substantiates the story of him being in a fight the night he died.

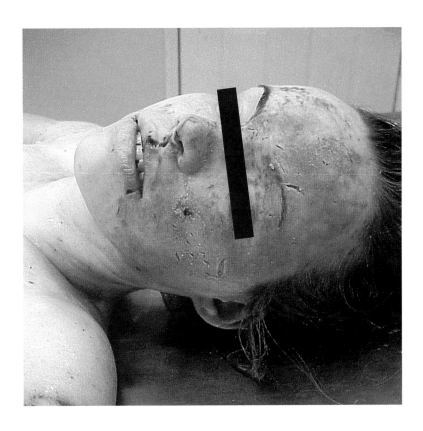

Photo 43. Numerous different facial injuries are common when a person hits the windshield in a traffic accident. This girl had contusions, abrasions, and lacerations. However, the external injuries she received do not prove she died of head trauma.

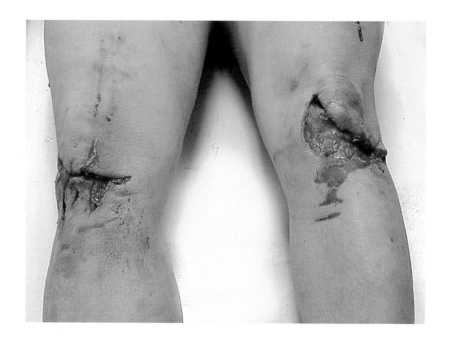

Photo 44. The injuries to this woman occurred when her legs were caught under the front seat of her car as she struck another vehicle.

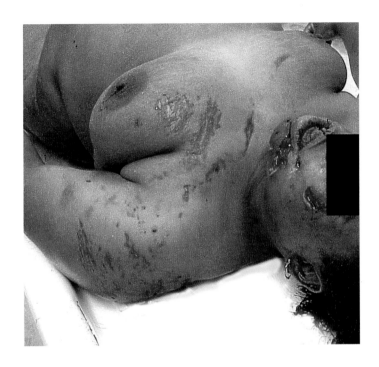

Photo 45. The injuries to this woman's breast and chest are "dicing" cuts or abrasions. These occurred when she came into contact with the side window.

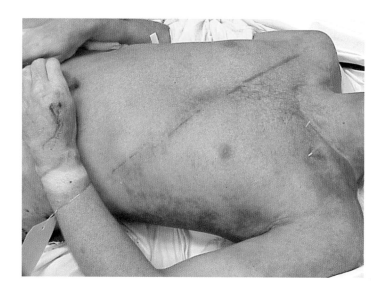

Photo 46. The abrasions on this man's chest were caused by a seat belt. The marks from the seatbelt on his right shoulder prove he was the passenger and not the driver.

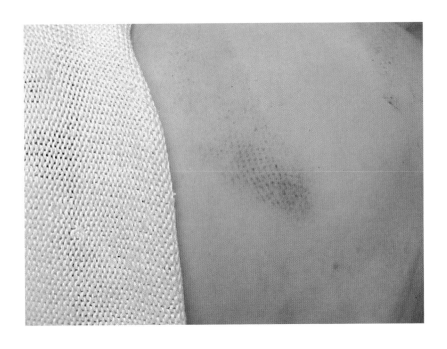

Photo 47. The pattern of this victim's clothing was left imprinted on her skin during a traffic accident.

Photo 48. This car was involved in a head-on collision with a motorcycle. *See next photo.*

Photo 49. The driver was saved by the airbag. *See next photo.*

Photo 50. The motorcycle following the accident. *See next photo.*

Photo 51. The man and woman on the motorcycle both died from multiple injuries to their heads, trunks, and extremities.

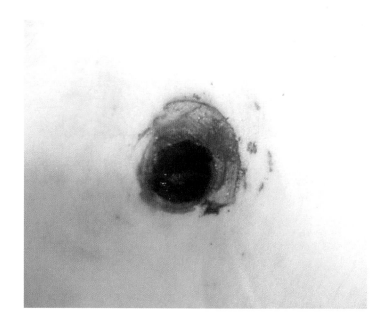

Photo 52. Contact gunshot wound. Abrasions from the muzzle of the gun and soot are present around the wound.

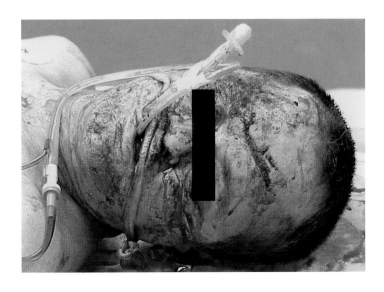

Photo 53. This man was thought to have been shot, but the wound was difficult to see before the head was cleaned. *See next photo.*

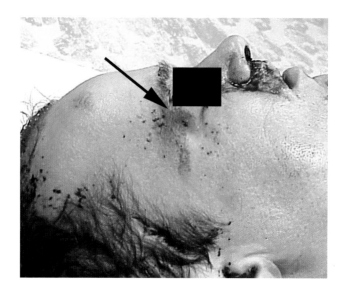

Photo 54. Cleaning the head revealed a close range gunshot wound adjacent to the right eye *(arrow)*.

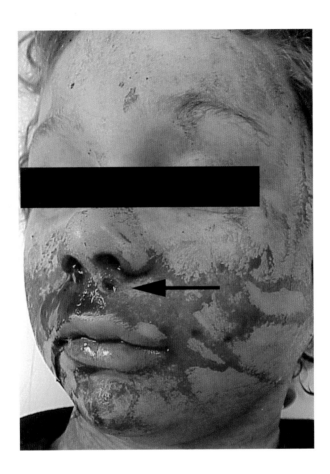

Photo 55. This boy was discovered dead in his bedroom. He was accidentally shot by his brother with a .22 caliber rifle *(arrow)*. *See next photo.*

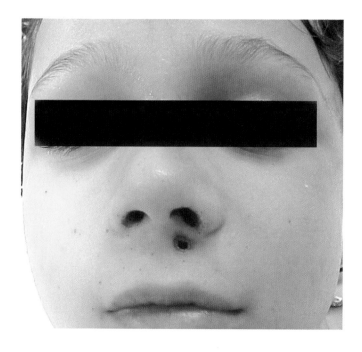

Photo 56. The presence of a few faint tattooing abrasions proves the distance of the rifle was such that the boy could not have accidentally shot himself.

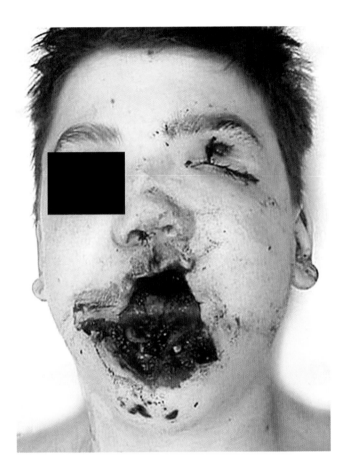

Photo 57. This 14-year-old boy went out hunting for the first time with his new rifle. He sat down with the gun and when he started to get up it discharged. Powder in the wound proves the gun barrel was near the mouth when the gun fired. The laceration in his left upper eyelid was caused by pressure from the bullet as it passed behind the eye.

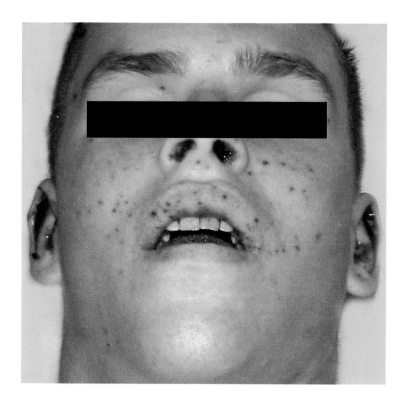

Photo 58. This young man was shot in the mouth. There is stippling around the mouth on the face proving this is an intermediate (medium) range wound.

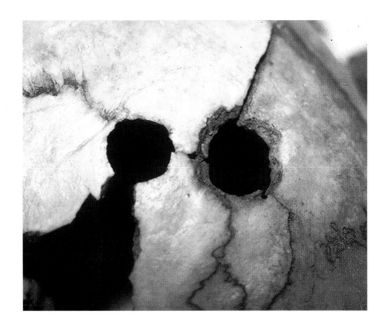

Photo 59. There are two gunshot wounds in this skull. The skull is formed by two plates of bone. As a bullet passes through these two plates, a larger defect with beveled edges will form on the exit side. In this case, the hole on the right is an exit wound and the one on the left is an entrance wound.

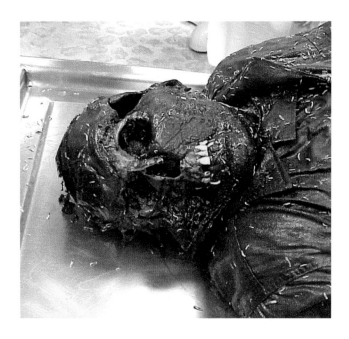

Photo 60. A soldier killed himself in the woods near his military base. He was markedly decomposed. There was no way to determine the entrance or exit wounds by looking at the skin. *See next photo.*

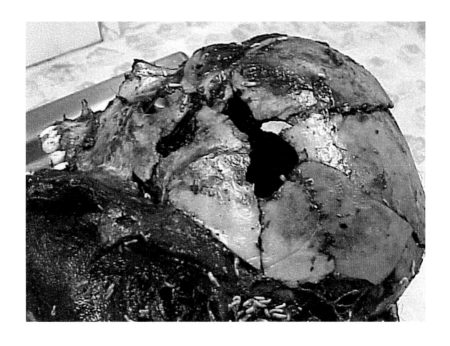

Photo 61. There were two defects, one on each side of the head. This side of the skull revealed sharp edges of the bone and no beveling, indicating it was the site of entrance. The defect on the other side had the beveled edges of an exit wound.

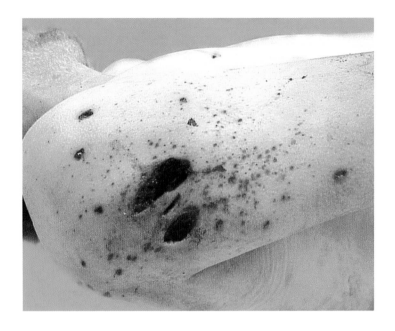

Photo 62. This man was shot with a rifle. The ragged entrance wound is surrounded by multiple defects. The bullet had passed through a car and fragments from the car caused these injuries.

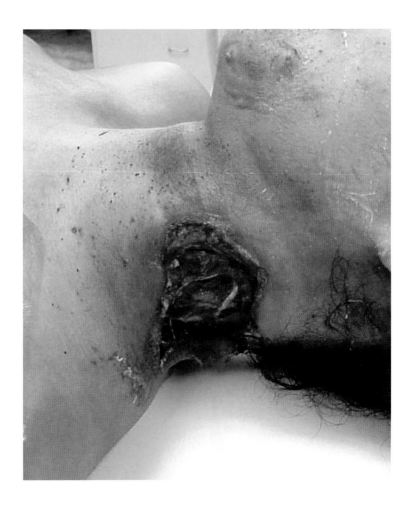

Photo 63. This woman was shot by a single projectile from a shotgun. The presence of powder around the wound indicates this was a close range shot. *See next photo.*

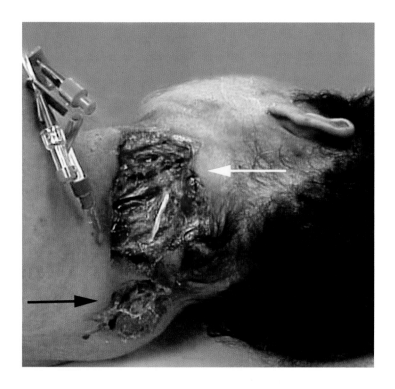

Photo 64. This view shows the entrance wound *(white arrow)* to be much larger than the exit wound *(black arrow)*. The projectile did not damage the major blood vessels, but the pressure caused injury to the woman's spinal cord. *See next photo.*

Photo 65. This is her spinal cord. The dark areas in the middle are dead tissue. Her cord was injured from the pressure of the blast and not from a direct hit. When she was shot, she dropped very suddenly. She was resuscitated, but never regained consciousness. There was little blood at the scene because her heart stopped suddenly after her spinal cord was damaged. *See next photo.*

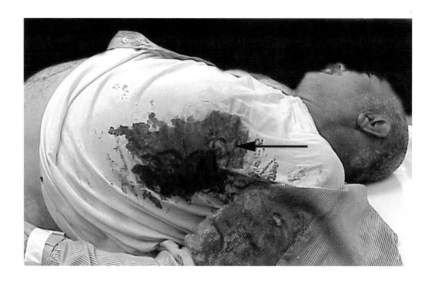

Photo 66. This man was shot during the same incident (see previous case).
He was shot in the chest with a shotgun slug *(arrow)*. *See next photo.*

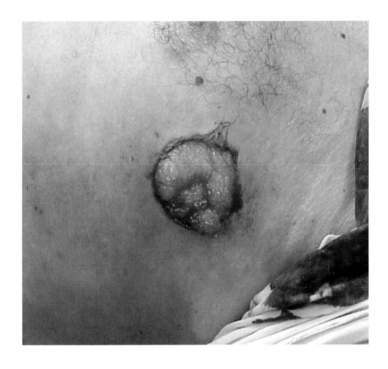

Photo 67. The entrance wound was a clean circular defect with fatty tissue in the wound. *See next photo.*

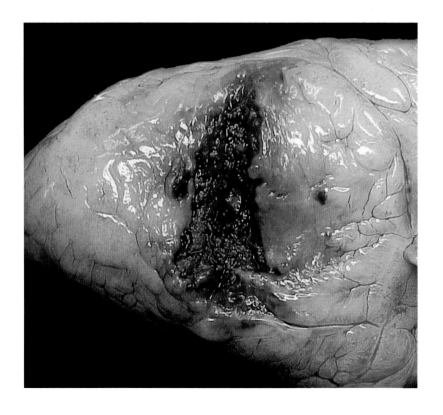

Photo 68. The shotgun slug caused a "gutter" wound of the heart. See next photo

Photo 69. This was the slug discovered in the man's right chest cavity. The single slug deformed into this unusually shaped projectile.

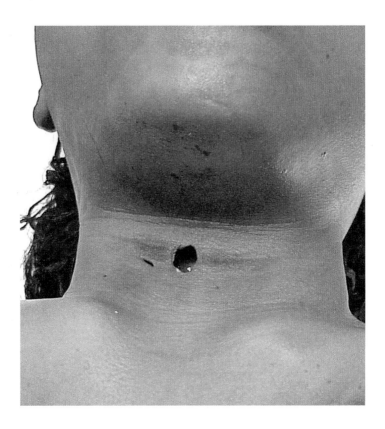

Photo 70. This woman died from a gunshot wound to the head. The wound in her neck was initially thought to be a gunshot wound; however, discussions with emergency room personnel revealed that it was a tracheotomy incision performed during CPR.

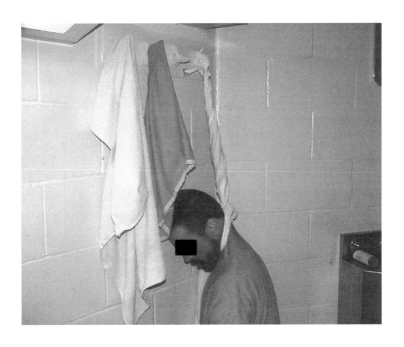

Photo 71. This man committed suicide while in jail. *See next photo.*

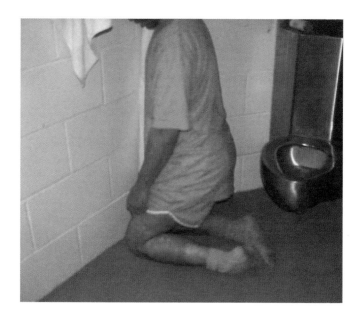

Photo 72. He was in contact with the floor. Contact with the floor is very common in suicidal hangings.

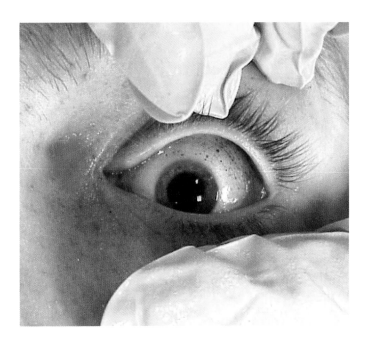

Photo 73. Petechiae (small pinpoint hemorrhages) of the eye that are characteristic of manual strangulation. They are also seen in sudden death, such as heart disease.

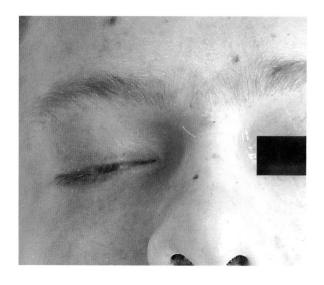

Photo 74. Petechiae may also be present on the skin of the face. There are faint petechiae on this boy's eyelid and below the eye.

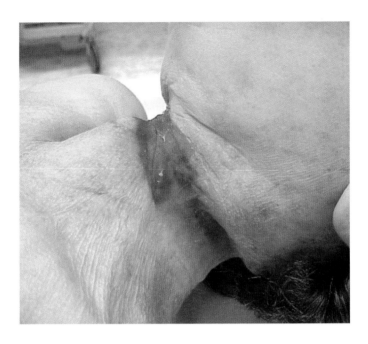

Photo 75. The ligature mark in this case was dried out. Dried ligature marks are more common the longer the body hangs prior to being discovered.

Photo 76. Farm accident. The tractor turned over after the driver attempted to navigate up the hill. The trailer, with a full load of rocks, pulled the tractor over. *See next photo.*

Photo 77. The driver was pinned under tractor. There were no significant injuries found at autopsy. He died from compression of the chest.

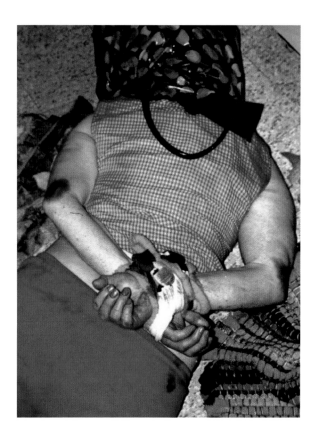

Photo 78. This woman was found dead in her kitchen. She was bound, beaten, and suffocated with a bag. The bruises on her elbows suggest she was forced to the floor while her hands were bound. The swelling of her hands proves the ligatures were on her wrists while she was alive.

Photo 79. This woman was discovered dead in her pool. *See next photo.*

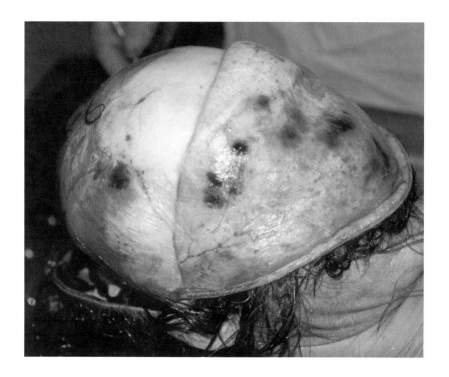

Photo 80. At autopsy, multiple subscalpular hemorrhages were discovered. The pathologist testified that these occurred from a fist, while the defendant said she obtained the injuries during rough sex. The jury convicted the defendant of murder.

Photo 81. Autoerotic death. This man was discovered dead in his bed. *See next photo*.

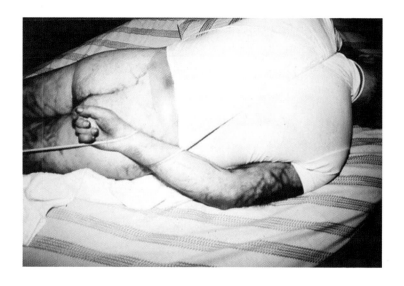

Photo 82. A rope was found around his neck, wrists, and legs. Moving his arm and legs would apply pressure to his neck in order to heighten his sexual pleasure.

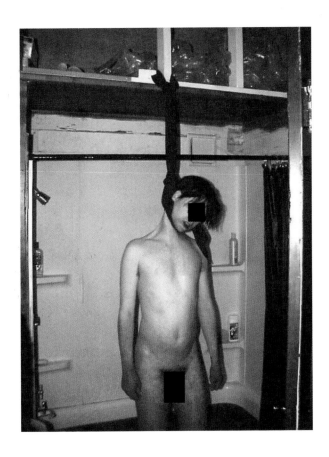

Photo 83. This young man hanged himself in his bathroom. An autoerotic accident was suspected because he was naked. *See next photo.*

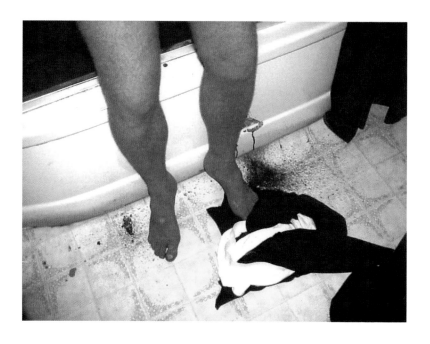

Photo 84. There was blood on the tub and the floor. *See next photo.*

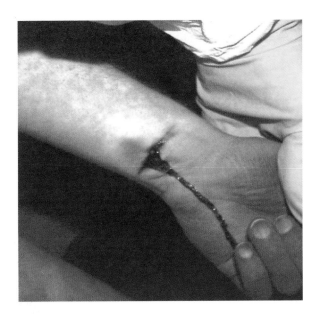

Photo 85. He had cut his wrist before hanging himself. *See next photo.*

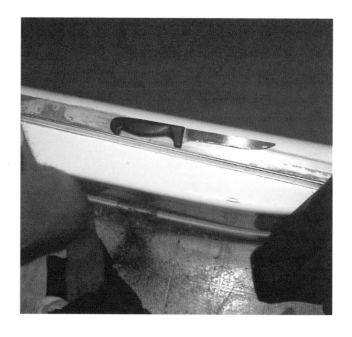

Photo 86. The knife was on the tub. His death was ruled a suicide.

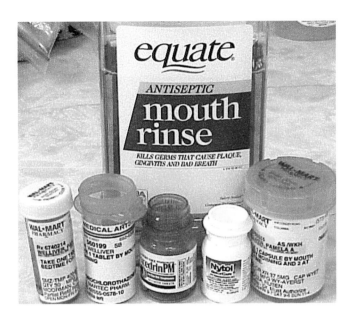

Photo 87. Many different types of drugs and medications cause overdoses. Investigators at a death scene should collect all drug-related items that may have played a role in a victim's death. The toxicologist needs to know all of the drugs that the decedent may have used.

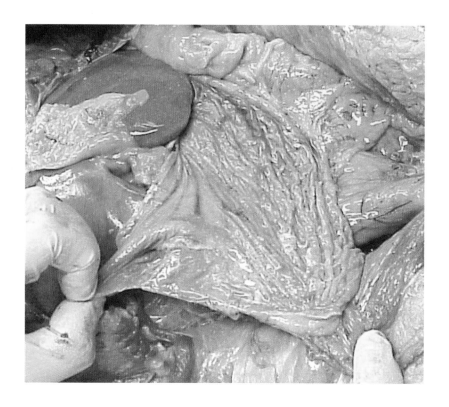

Photo 88. This green material was lining the stomach of a person who over-dosed. *See next photo.*

Photo 89. The liquid material was recovered from the stomach and sent to the toxicologist for analysis.

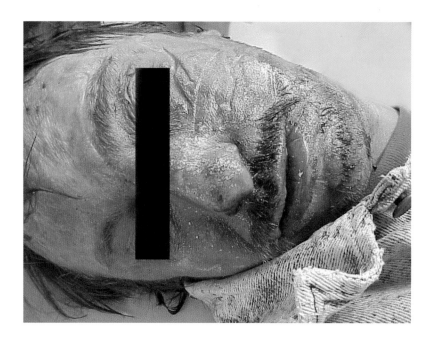

Photo 90. The gold paint around this man's face came from a can of Rustoleum that was sprayed into a bag and then inhaled. He died of asphyxiation.

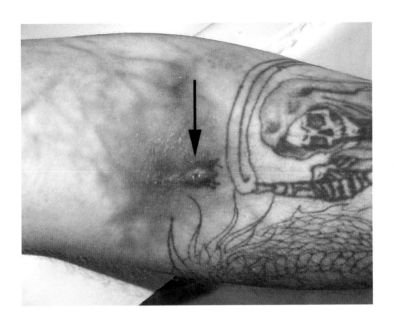

Photo 91. Some drug abusers hide their injection sites in tattoos.

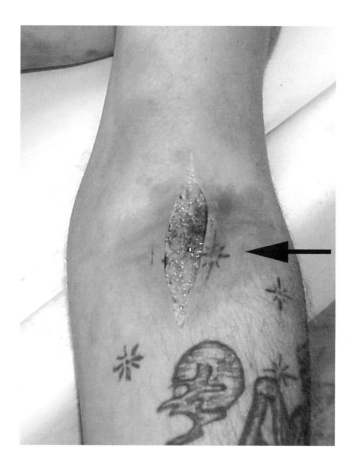

Photo 92. The pathologist may incise the arm to check for recent bleeding from an injection site.

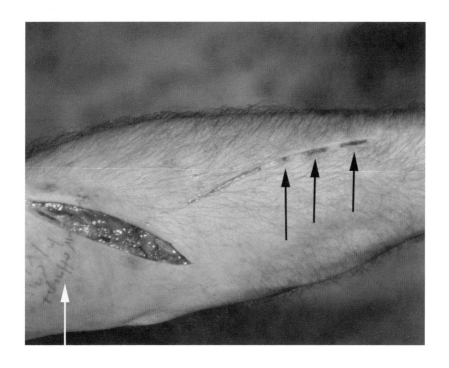

Photo 93. There were multiple injection sites *(black arrows)* in this drug abuser's arm. The *white arrow* points to writing that emergency room personnel wrote to tell the pathologist which needle punctures they had made.

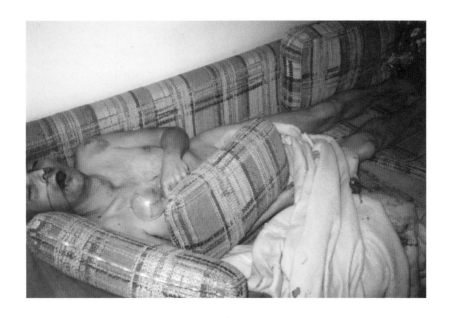

Photo 94. This naked man was lying dead on his couch. He was still holding onto a glass. *See next photo.*

Photo 95. There were numerous blood-filled containers next to his body. *See next photo.*

Photo 96. There was blood in the bathtub. *See next photo.*

Photo 97. Blood and a syringe were also present in the kitchen sink. *See next photo.*

Photo 98. He had deposited his empty bottles behind the couch. The autopsy revealed cirrhosis of the liver, abundant blood vessel in his gastrointestinal tract, and a positive drug screen for alcohol. A blood vessel had ruptured in his esophagus as a complication of his liver disease.

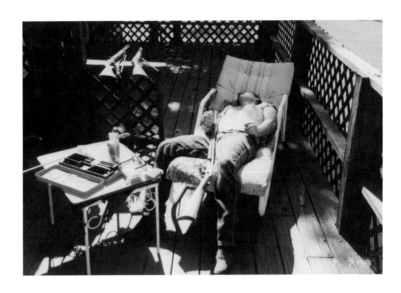

Photo 99. This man was found dead on his back deck. It appeared as if he was cleaning his rifle and it had discharged. *See next photo.*

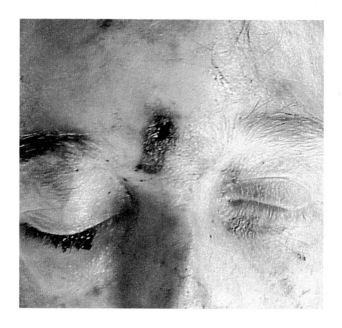

Photo 100. He died from a loose contact gunshot wound to his forehead. The wound looked more like a suicide wound than one caused by an accident. *See next photo.*

Photo 101. There were cleaning supplies on the table next to him. *See next photo.*

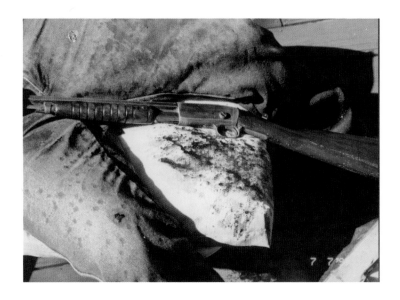

Photo 102. The rifle was discovered between his legs. Examination of the rifle revealed that it would discharge if the butt had struck a hard surface (such as the deck). The man was not known to be suicidal and had just spoken with his wife. His death was ruled an accident.

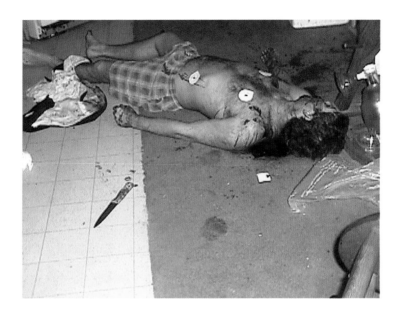

Photo 103. This man was stabbed twice in the chest by his girlfriend during a fight. The scene photograph shows the location of one of two knives used in the homicide. The location of weapons at the scene may aid the pathologist in determining which knife caused which wound.

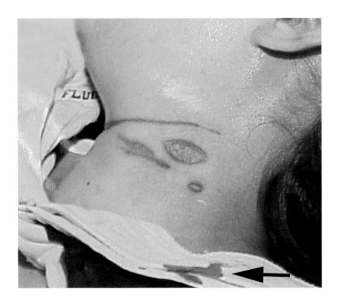

Photo 104. This woman was killed by a gunshot wound to the head. The incised wounds to her neck were made after death. There was a slight amount of bleeding from one of the wounds. The blood is visible on her shirt.

Photo 105. This man was lying in a "circle" of blood. *See next photo.*

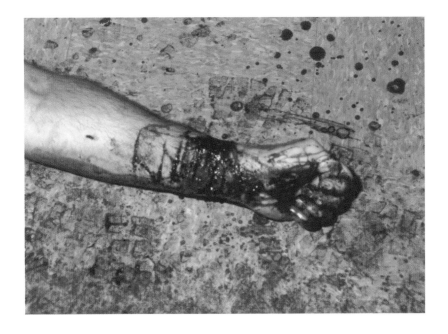

Photo 106. He had cut his left wrist numerous times. The pattern of the blood spatters showed that he had walked in a counterclockwise direction until he fell.

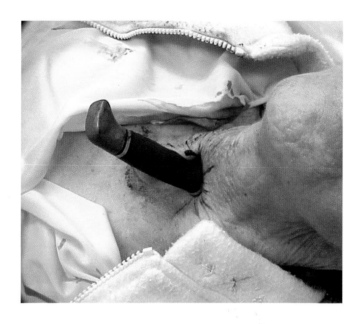

Photo 107. This woman was discovered lying on the floor. Her walker was overturned nearby. When she was rolled over, a knife was discovered in her neck. It had been driven down to the hilt. *See next photo.*

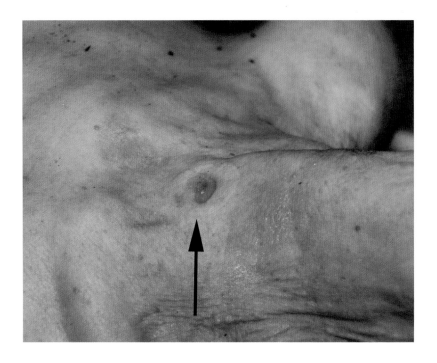

Photo 108. There were no injuries around the stab wound *(arrow)*, suggesting the knife was thrust in with a single motion. The woman could have been stabbed, or she could have fallen on the knife.

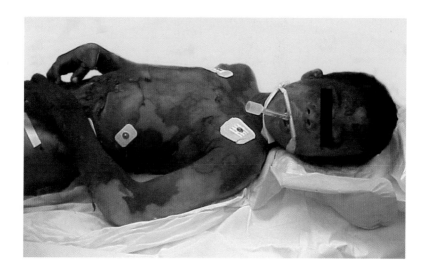

Photo 109. Thermal injuries. This boy died during resuscitation. The red discoloration of his skin suggests carbon monoxide inhalation or change in color due to the heat. Examination of the neck would reveal if he had inhaled smoke.

Photo 110. Splits of the skin are common artifacts of thermal injury.

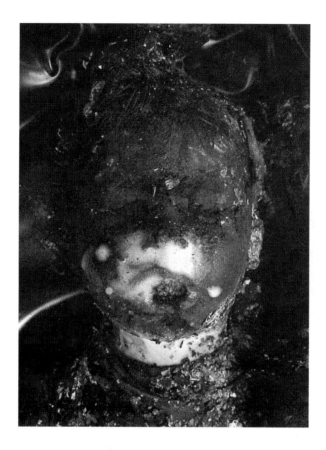

Photo 111. The foam in this boy's nose indicates he was alive at the time of the fire.

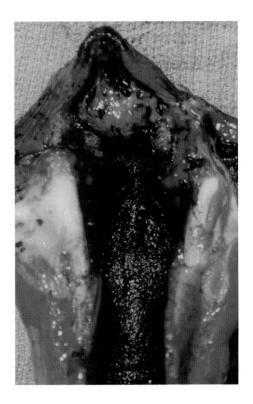

Photo 112. Soot in a fire victim's airway. This proved the person was alive during the fire.

Photo 113. This boy died in a fire. The bleeding under the skull (epidural hemorrhage) is an artifact of the fire and not the result of blunt impact injury.

Photo 114. A truck ran over this man's car. He was killed instantly when his neck was fractured. *See next photo.*

Photo 115. His son was lying curled up in the back seat. He usually slept in this position when he was in the car. He died from carbon monoxide poisoning after inhaling smoke. His position and the presence of significant injuries to his head suggest he was unconscious at the time he was breathing in the smoke.

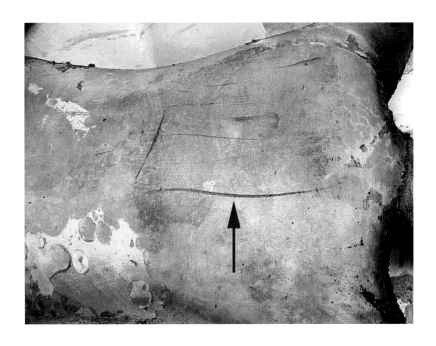

Photo 116. These superficial incised wounds on this woman's back were suspicious. Discussions with firemen who had been at the scene revealed she
was dragged out of the building over broken glass that was on the floor.

Photo 117. This woman died of hypothermia during the winter after falling down on her porch. She could not get up due to chronic, severe arthritis. *See next photo.*

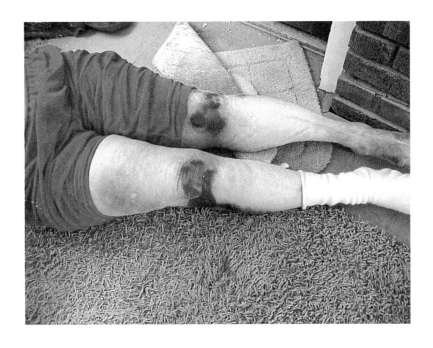

Photo 118. Abrasions on her knees and feet revealed she struggled after falling. Autopsy did not reveal any other causes of death. *See next photo.*

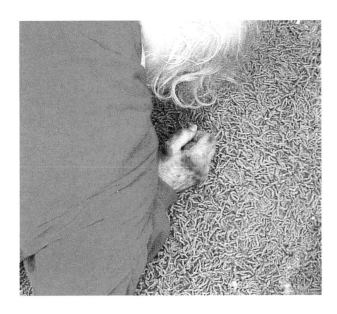

Photo 119. There were also abrasions on her hands.

Photo 120. This woman died while she was sunbathing. *See next photo.*

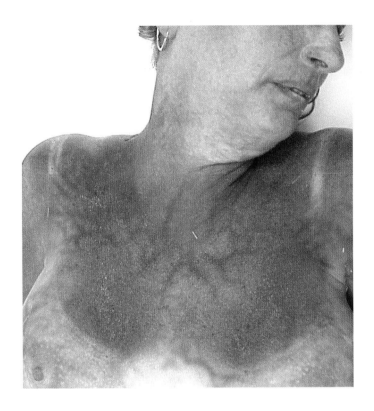

Photo 121. Her autopsy was negative except for decompositional changes and a blood alcohol of 0.35 grams/dL. She could have died either from hyperthermia, acute and chronic alcohol intoxication, or a combination of the two. *See next photo.*

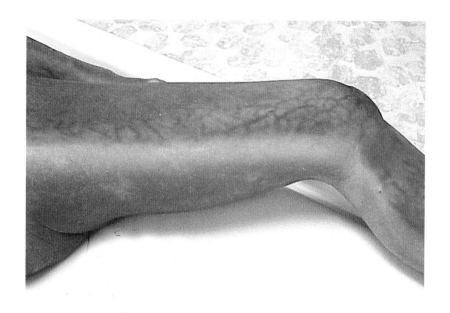

Photo 122. In addition to signs of decomposition, the sun-exposed skin had turned gray. This is a postmortem "tan." *See next photo.*

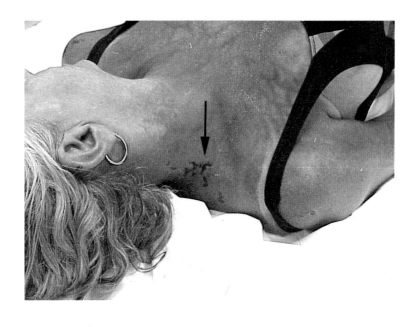

Photo 123. There was also evidence of postmortem insect activity *(arrow)*.

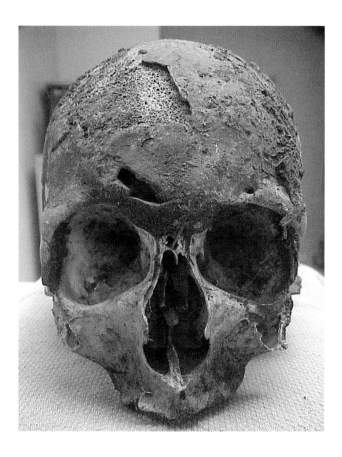

Photo 124. This skull was discovered in a burned-out culvert. *See next photo.*

Photo 125. There is a large open defect on the left side. Was this due to the fire or to an injury? *See next photo.*

Photo 126. A closer view of the defect *(arrow)* reveals an antemortem injury. A weapon like a machete or an ax caused this cleaved-out defect.

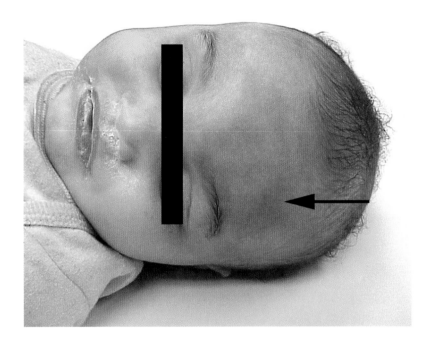

Photo 127. Bruises *(arrow)* on the head of a child who is not old enough to walk must be explained. It was determined that the babysitter struck this child.

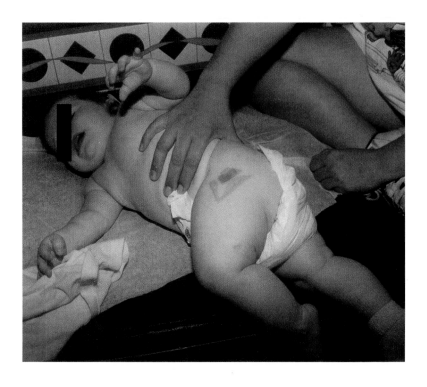

Photo 128. This child was intentionally burned on his hip. *See next photo.*

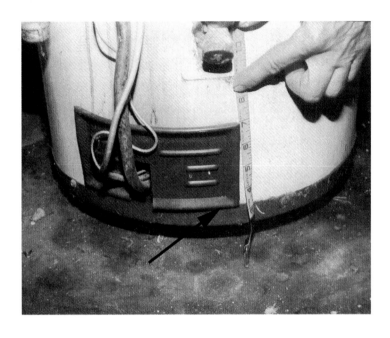

Photo 129. This is the water heater located in the basement of the residence. It was determined that the child was pressed against it, causing the burn. The *arrow* points to the part of the furnace against which the child was pressed.

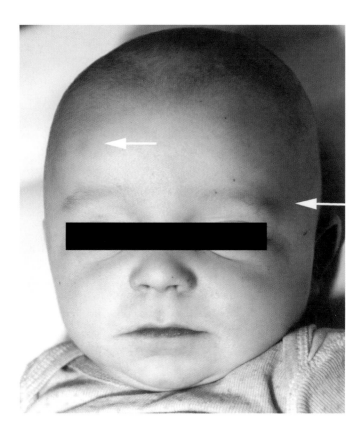

Photo 130. This 3-week-old baby was discovered dead in his crib. The other members of the family present in the house included two female siblings, ages 3 and 4, and their father. The baby had bruises on his face *(arrows)*. *See next photo.*

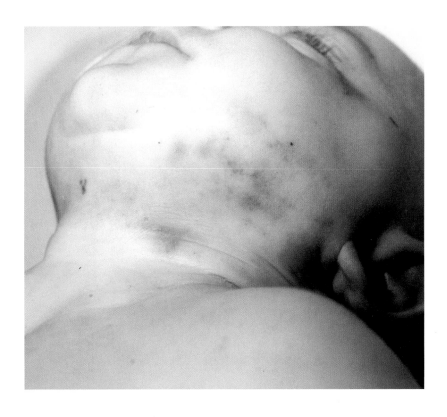

Photo 131. There were a few abrasions and numerous bruises on the baby's neck. The bruises were quite small. *See next photo.*

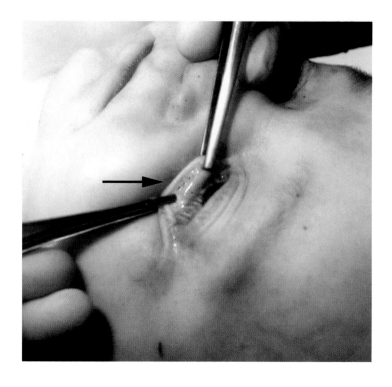

Photo 132. There were petechiae *(arrow)* in both eyes. *See next photo.*

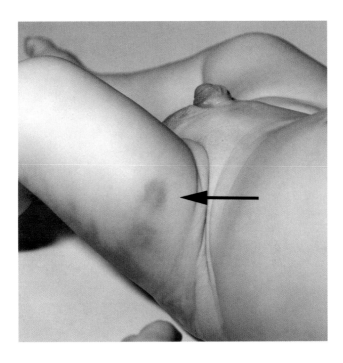

Photo 133. There was a pinch mark on his left thigh *(arrow)*. The mark was too small to have been made by his father. *See next photo.*

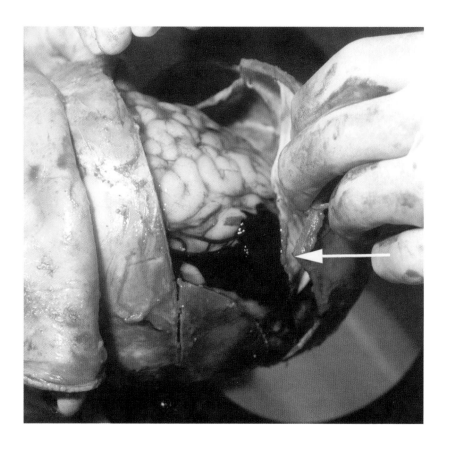

Photo 134. He also had a subdural hemorrhage that indicated a blow to the head. Two weeks before the infant died, the mother discovered one of the siblings choking him. The history and the injuries pointed to the 3-year-old as the culprit.

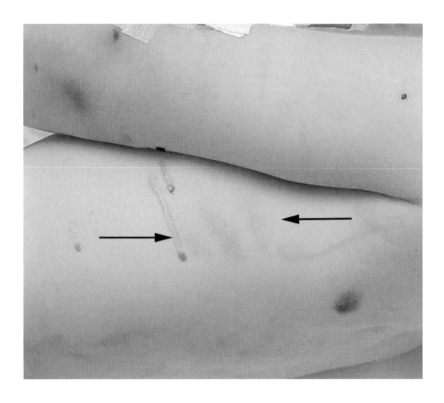

Photo 135. This child had been grabbed by the chest and shaken. The finger mark contusions are easy to see *(arrows)*. External injuries may or may not be present in infants who are shaken.

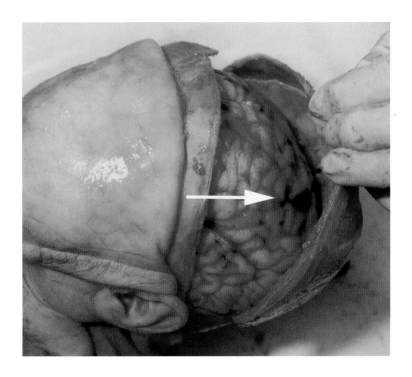

Photo 136. Shaken infants may have subarachnoid and subdural hemor-rhages. This child has some subarachnoid hemorrhage *(arrow)*. *See next photo.*

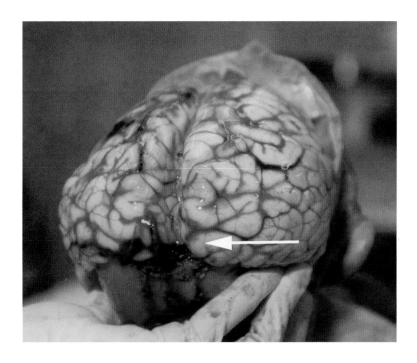

Photo 137. The same child also had a collection of blood (subdural hemorrhage) at the back of the head *(arrow)*. *See next photo.*

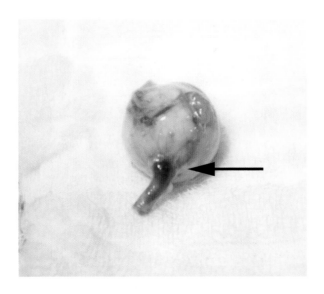

Photo 138. There were also optic nerve hemorrhages *(arrow)* at the back of his eyes. Retinal hemorrhage was seen in the eye when it was cut open and examined.

Photo 139. This child was exhumed 9 years after he was killed. No autopsy had been performed following his death. The hospital records indicated a skull fracture and retinal hemorrhages. *See next photo.*

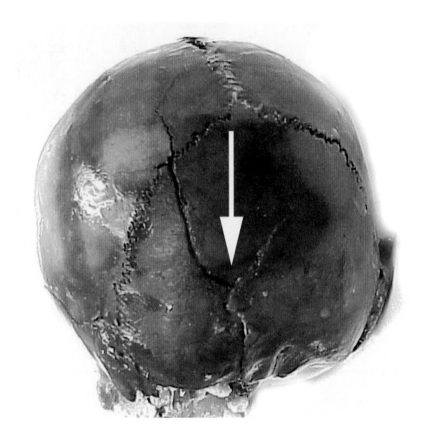

Photo 140. Only the skull fracture *(arrow)* could be diagnosed after the exhumation because the body was too decomposed to see any other injuries. The presence of the skull fracture and the history of retinal hemorrhages led to a murder charge.

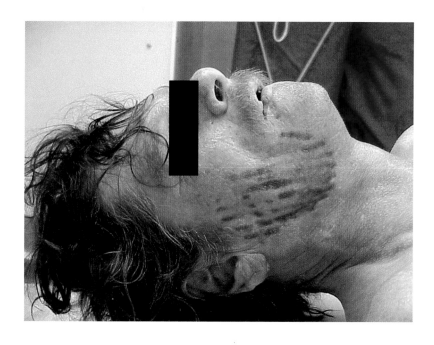

Photo 141. This man was electrocuted when he came into contact with over six thousand volts. There is a burn pattern on his face that came from a truck he was standing next to. *See next photo.*

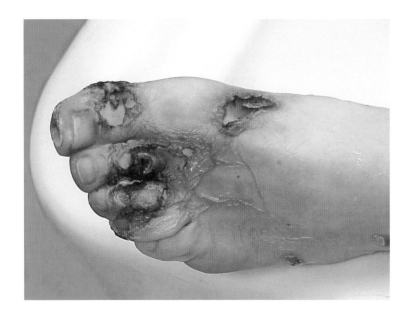

Photo 142. He had burn marks on his left foot and not on his right. *See next photo.*

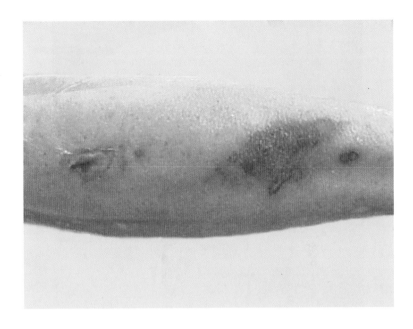

Photo 143. The burn marks on his right arm appeared different than the burns on his foot. The burns do not always appear similarly. *See next photo.*

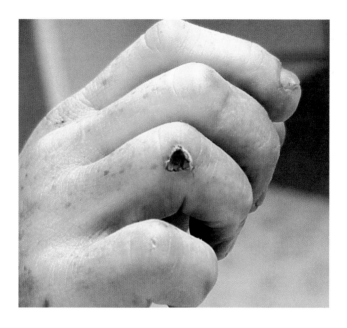

Photo 144. This solitary burn mark on his right hand is similar to the smaller burns seen in lower voltage injuries.

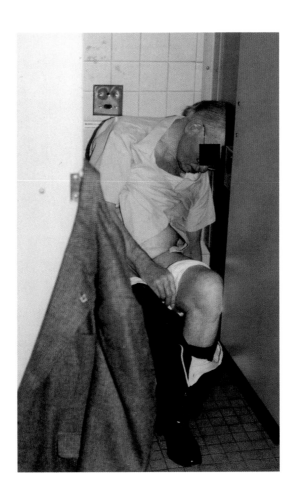

Photo 145. This man died suddenly while using the toilet. He had a history of heart problems. People with heart disease can die suddenly at any time; however, dying suddenly on the toilet is not an uncommon occurrence.

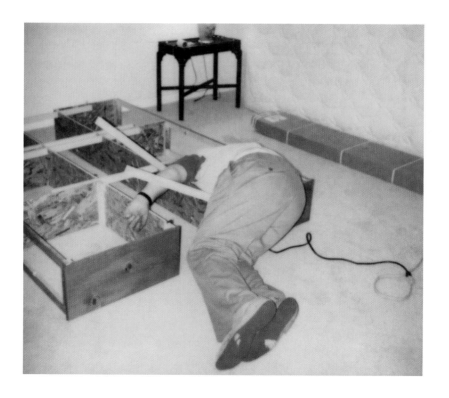

Photo 146. The most common cause of sudden death is heart disease. When either an electrical appliance or cord is present, electrocution must be ruled out as a cause of death. *See next photo.*

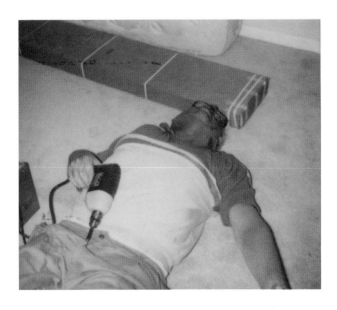

Photo 147. The man was working with an electric tool. If the autopsy had not confirmed a cause of death, the tool must be tested to make sure it did not cause or contribute to his death.

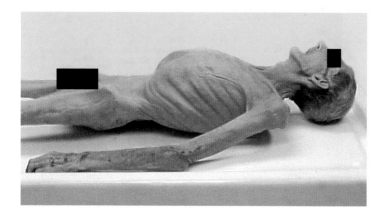

Photo 148. Chronic disease may cause a person to become emaciated. The diagnosis of starvation is usually made by visual inspection because there is no laboratory test that proves a person died of malnutrition. If there is an underlying disease, such as cancer, it will be apparent at the autopsy.

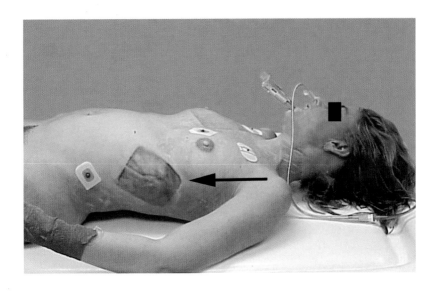

Photo 149. Injuries from CPR are common. The rectangular-shaped abrasion *(arrow)* on this young woman's chest was caused by an electrocardioversion (shock) attempt.

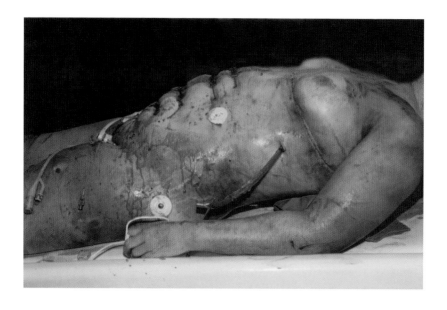

Photo 150. There may be many injuries that are altered or difficult to see because of recent therapy or hospitalization. This woman had been shot in the chest with a shotgun and the bullet traveled down into her abdomen. The surgery prevented an accurate description of the damage done by the pellets. The pellets were recovered.

APPENDIX

MEDICAL TERMINOLOGY

A

Acquired — not born with, developed after birth

Adenoma — a benign tumor made up of glandular elements

Adhesion — fibrous tissue (scarring) that connects one structure to another as a response to disease or injury

Alopecia — loss of hair

Alveoli — air sacs in the lungs

Ambulatory — able to walk

Anamnestic — history

Anastomosis — a joining together

Aneurysm — an out-pouching of a blood vessel or structure

Angina pectoris — chest pain without death of the heart muscle

Angiography — an x-ray study of blood vessels by dye

Anoxia — no oxygen

Antecubital fossa — the space on the arm in front of the elbow

Antemortem — before death

Anterior — in front of

Anthracosis — black pigment from coal or cigarette smoke

Anthropophagia — insect and animal eating of the body after death

Arrhythmia — abnormal heart beat

Arteriolonephosclerosis — small blood vessel disease of the kidney

Artery — a blood vessel that takes blood away from the heart

Arteriosclerosis — thickening of artery walls, "hardening of the arteries"

Ascites — accumulation of fluid in the abdomen

Asphyxia — lack of oxygen in the blood

Atelectasis — collapse of a lung

Atherosclerosis — thickening of artery walls by fatty deposits

Atrium — one of two chambers in the heart that accepts blood from either the lungs or the rest of the body

Atrophy — wasting away
Autolysis — degeneration of cells and tissues after death

B

Benzoylecognine — a metabolite of cocaine
Bifurcation — a division into two branches
Bronchi — the breathing tubes between the trachea and the lungs
Bronchioles — smaller divisions of the bronchi
Bronchopneumonia — infection of the lung beginning in the bronchiole (smallest air tube)

C

Calcification — turning hard by the development of calcium
Cancer — malignant growth
Capillary — the smallest blood vessel that connects arteries and veins
Carbohydrates — starches and sugars
Cardiac — heart
Cardiac tamponade — blood filling the pericardial sac and compressing the heart
Cardiomegaly — increased size of the heart
Cardiomyopathy — abnormality of the heart wall
Cardiorespiratory — heart and lungs
Cardiovascular — heart and blood vessels
Cecum — the first part of the large bowel (colon) where the small bowel attaches and the appendix is located
Cerebral — brain
Cholecystectomy — surgical removal of the gallbladder
Cholelithiasis — gallstones
Chordae tendineae — the strings of tissue connecting the heart valves to the papillary muscles in the heart wall
Cirrhosis — scarring of the liver complicating alcoholism
Colon — the large bowel, between the small bowel and the anus
Coma — unresponsive condition
Congenital — born with
Congestion — accumulation of blood

Conjunctiva — the thin membrane lining the eyelid and eyeball
Connective tissue — the supporting tissue between structures
Consolidation — becoming firm
Contrecoup — opposite the point of impact
Coronal — the plane across the body from side to side
Coup — at the point of impact
Cutaneous — skin
Cyanosis — the dusky discoloration of the skin due to a lack of oxygen
Cyst — a hollow structure with a lining that is filled with a liquid or a semiliquid substance

D
Decubitus ulcer — an ulcer formed on the skin from pressure
Dementia — loss of intellectual function
Dermatome — the distribution of a nerve on the exterior of the body
Diabetes mellitus — a disease in which the body cannot use sugar because insulin is not being adequately produced by the pancreas
Diastolic — the lower of the two values in a blood pressure
Dilated — expanded in size
Distal — away from the point of insertion
DNA (deoxyribonucleic acid) — the structural backbone of genetic makeup in chromosomes
Duodenum — the first part of the small bowel
Dura mater — the tough, thick membrane located between the brain and the skull

E
–ectomy — excision of
Ecchymoses — hemorrhages beneath the skin (larger than petechiae)
Ecstasy (methylenedioxymethamphetamine) — a recreational drug of abuse
Edema — the accumulation of fluid in cells and tissues
Electrocardioversion — an attempt at cardiopulmonary resuscitation by electrical shock
Emaciation — generalized wasting away

Emphysema — lung disease where there is retention of air because of damage to the alveoli (air sacs)

Endometrium — the inner lining of the uterus

Epidural — in between the dura and the skull

Esophagus — the structure connecting the mouth to the stomach (food pipe)

Etiology — the cause of a disease

Exsanguination — marked internal or external loss of blood

F

Fibrillation — very rapid irregular heart beat

Fibrosis — scarring, commonly associated with liver and the heart

Flexion — the act of bending a structure

Forensic pathology — the legal applications to the field of pathology, study of the cause and manner of death and injury

Foramen magnum — the hole at the base of the skull through which the spinal cord passes

G

Gastrocnemius — the calf muscle

GHB (gamma hydroxybutarate) — a date-rape drug that can cause sudden death.

Gland — a structure made up of cells that secrete a substance

Glucose — sugar

Granular — a "lumpy bumpy" surface

Granuloma — a tumor-like growth caused by an infection

H

Hematoma — a mass (collection) of blood

–hemo — blood

Hepatomegaly — increased size of the liver

Hepatic — pertaining to the liver

Herniation — the protrusion of a structure into another space

Hyperglycemia — increased sugar (glucose) in the blood

Hyperplastic — increased number

Hypertension — high blood pressure

Hyperthermia — increased body temperature
Hypertrophy — enlargement
Hypothermia — decreased body temperature
Hypoglycemia — decreased sugar (glucose) in the blood
Hysterectomy — surgical removal of the uterus

I
Ileum — the third and most distal part of the small bowel
Infarction — death of tissue from a lack of blood
Inferior — below
Inflammation — infection
Infraorbital — below the eye
Intercostal — between the ribs
Interstitial tissue — the supporting tissue within an organ, not the functioning cell
Intestines — the bowels
Intima — the innermost structure
Ischemia — decreased blood flow
–itis — inflammation

J
Jaundice — yellow discoloration of the skin from a buildup of bilirubin (a breakdown product of red blood cells) in the body
Jejunum — the second part of the small bowel

L
Laparotomy — surgical incision into the abdomen
Larynx — voice box (contains the vocal cords)
Leukemia — cancer of the blood-forming organs and cells
Ligament — thick tissue joining bones and cartilage
Liver mortis — settling of blood after death
Lumen — the inside of a hollow organ or blood vessel
Lymph — the clear fluid that drains from the body's tissues
Lymphoma — cancer of the lymph system
Lymph node — nodules of tissue along the lymph drainage system

M
Mastectomy — surgical removal of the breast
Mastoid — the area of the skull behind the ear
Media — the middle layer of a blood vessel
Medial — the middle
Membrane — the lining tissue within a structure or between two structures
Meningitis — inflammation of the coverings of the brain
Mesentery — the structure that supports the intestines
Metabolite — a breakdown product of a drug or chemical
Mitral valve — the valve between the left atrium and ventricle in the heart
Myocardium — heart muscle
Myocardial infarct — death of the heart muscle from the blockage of a coronary artery
Myocarditis — inflammation (infection) of the heart wall

N
Necrosis — degeneration and death of cells and tissues during life
Neoplasia — tumor or growth
Nodules — raised skin lesions, may be benign or malignant

O
Oophorectomy — surgical removal of the ovary

P
Pancreas — the organ behind the stomach that produces insulin
Papillary muscles — muscle bundles that control the heart valves
Parenchyma — the functional tissue of an organ
Penetration — into a structure
Perforation — through a structure
Pericardial sac — the sac surrounding the heart
Perineum — the area of the body that includes the external genitalia and the anus
Peritoneal cavity — abdominal cavity

Peritoneum — the thick tissue lining the abdominal cavity
Perivascular — around blood vessels
Petechiae — pinpoint hemorrhages
Pharynx — the structure at the back of the nose and mouth before the esophagus and larynx
Pinna — the external ear
Pleura — lining the lung or inside the chest
Pleural space — space between the lung and the chest wall
Posterior — behind or back
Postmortem — after death
Prone — lying on the front
Proximal — toward the point of insertion or the main part of the body
Purging — the decomposed bodily fluids which come out the nose and mouth

R
Renal — kidney
Rigor mortis — stiffening of the muscles after death

S
Sagittal — a plane across the body from front to back
Salpingo-oopherectomy — surgical removal of the fallopian tubes and the ovaries
Sarcoma — a malignant tumor of the soft tissue
Septicemia — bacteria in the blood system with signs and symptoms of disease
Shock — inadequate circulating blood volume because of either a loss or redistribution of blood
Small bowel — the small intestine, extends from the stomach to the colon (large bowel)
Soft tissue — fat or supporting tissue
Splenectomy — surgical removal of the spleen
Stenosis — narrowing
Subarachnoid — beneath the arachnoid
Subcutaneous marbling — the black discoloration of the blood vessels on the outside of the body that appears during decomposition

Subdural — beneath the dura

Subluxation — bones that partially slip out of joint

Superior — above

Supine — lying on the back with face upward

Supraorbital — above the eye

Suture — joints in the skull where the bones come together

Syncope — fainting

Systolic — the higher of the two valves in a blood pressure

T

Tachycardia — fast heart beat

Tardieu spots — small hemorrhages from ruptured blood vessels on the extremities that occur after the body has been in a dependent position

Thoracic cavity — chest cavity

Thoracotomy — surgical incision into the chest cavity

Thorax — chest

Trachea — (wind pipe) the structure between the larynx (voice box) and the bronchi

Tricuspid valve — the valve between the right atrium and right ventricle in the heart

U

Ureter — the structure that takes urine from the kidney to the urinary bladder

V

Varix (varices) — enlarged dilated vein from a backup of blood; seen in alcoholics who have cirrhosis of the liver

Vein — a blood vessel that returns blood to the heart

Ventricle — a chamber containing either blood or fluid (e.g., the heart has two ventricular chambers)

Vitreous humor — the fluid in the eye that gives the eye its shape